Introduction
to Clothing
Production
Managem

Introduction to Clothing Production Management

Second Edition

A.J. Chuter
Wrenbury Associates, Leeds

Blackwell
Science

Blackwell Science Ltd,
a Blackwell Publishing company
Editorial offices:
Blackwell Science Ltd, 9600 Garsington Road,
Oxford OX4 2DQ, UK
  Tel: +44 (0) 1865 776868
Blackwell Publishing Professional, 2121 State
Avenue, Ames, Iowa 50014-8300, USA
  Tel: +1 515 292 0140
Blackwell Science Asia Pty, 550 Swanston Street,
Carlton, Victoria 3053, Australia
  Tel: +61 (0)3 8359 1011

First edition published 1988
Reprinted 1990
Second edition published 1995
4   2007

Library of Congress Cataloging-in-Publication Data
is available

ISBN: 978-0-632-03939-5

A catalogue record for this title is available from the
British Library

For further information on Blackwell Publishing,
visit our website:
www.blackwellpublishing.com

Contents

Acknowledgements   ix
Introduction   xi

1 THE SEWING ROOM SUPERVISOR   1
Introduction   1
The supervisor's job   2
Sample of a list of supervisory duties   6
Factory routine   8
Supervisor training needs   10
Supervisor's check list   11

2 HOW OUTPUT IS LOST   13
Introduction   13
Work content   15
Improving profitability   18
Calculating how much output is lost   20

3 BASIC METHOD STUDY   23
Introduction   23
Method Study's part in your job   26
Sequence of improvement   27
Principles of motion economy   29
How to record methods   30
Practical aspects   34
Check list   36

4 BASIC WORK MEASUREMENT   37
Introduction   37
Work Measurement: its part in your job   38
Watches   40

Elements   41
Timing   44
Timing errors   46
Rating   47
Allowances   49
Standard time calculation   51
Predetermined motion time systems (PMTS)   53

5 BALANCING   55
Introduction   55
Basics   57
Theoretical balance   59
Skills inventory   61
Initial balance   62
Exercise   66
Balance control   66
Guidelines for supervisors   71

6 BALANCING EXERCISES   72
Introduction   72
Exercise 1   72
Exercise 2   74
Exercise 3   76
Exercise 4   76
Exercise 5   77

7 PRODUCTION SYSTEMS, PLANNING AND CONTROL   94
Production systems   94
Production planning and control   102

8 TOTAL QUALITY CONTROL   111
Introduction   111
Terms in use   112
The Quality Control Department   114
NACERAP   118
ISO 9000 and TQM   119

9 QUALITY FROM DESIGN TO DESPATCH   122
Introduction   122
Design   123
Cloth and trimmings   124
Fusibles   127
Cutting   128
Making up   134
After make   138
The quality cycle   141

10   PRODUCTION AND PEOPLE   142
Introduction   142
A basic guide to supervising people   143
Leading groups of people   145
Communication   148
Discipline   150

11   TRAINING   154
Introduction   154
How people learn   155
Putting training to work   158
Leadership training   161
Leader/subordinate analysis   163
The training plan for supervisors   166
Training check list   166

12   CHARTING AND LAYOUTS   167
Introduction   167
Analysis by means of charts   168
Layout   171
Exercise 1   176
Exercise 2   179

Reading List   185
Index   187

Acknowledgements

Chief thanks are due to Norman Slater, a former colleague in the Clothing and Allied Products Industry Training Board, for his thorough reading of the manuscript, together with his lively and well informed comments. The book is partly based on the lecture notes which were written by the author for the Production Management Training Courses run for that ITB and which were honed on the comment of the Production Team who, in addition to Norman Slater, included Paul Gauntlett, Mike Locke and Ted Triggs.

The author first learned much of what is in this book as an employee of Kurt Salmon Associates and owes a great deal to the advice of John Beddows and Roger Fielding, who were his supervisors for much of his service.

Various chapters were revised and amended as a result of comment from friends in the industry, the Northern Ireland ITB and the colleges, together with colleagues from Leeds and Salford Universities.

Introduction

The nature of the book

Industry

The text is concerned with the basic tools of production management, the tools of supervision. It concentrates on the short-term problems, like meeting today's targets. It is structured so that it can form the basis of a supervisors' or junior managers' course. Indeed, such courses are often run by production managers and few are qualified trainers so it is worded almost as it might be delivered, as a series of lectures. The text is interspersed with catch-phrases which have proved to be memorable in various parts of the world.

Technical education

It is also intended to fill a gap in the literature which is available for students taking the National Diploma in Clothing and, as background, for those taking higher but non-clothing studies. It has also proved to be useful to students of Textile Technology.

Scope

The book assumes very little previous knowledge of the subject and has been kept to a reasonable size by asking the following questions:

- What is the knowledge which is essential at this level?
- What is contained in books which are widely available but which cover general industry?
- What is available, free of charge, especially from the thread, needle and fusible suppliers?

The sewing room supervisor

The book is partly intended as a manual for supervisors and so it starts with a chapter on the job, the sewing room being selected as an example because that is where supervisors work. What are the key parts of their work? How much time should and do they spend in each activity? Why is there a discrepancy and what can be done about it?

How output is lost

In this chapter we examine the human resources provided in the sewing room and see how these are frittered away because of poor training, labour turnover, absenteeism, unplanned balancing, inadequate Work Study and a low standard of machine reliability.

Basic Work Study

Work Study has two important implications for the training of production staff:

- the emphasis that it places on a logical approach to problems;
- its two main branches, Method Study and Work Measurement, are fundamental to most scientific approaches to clothing production management.

Method Study is typified by the slogan 'There has to be a better way'. In a labour-intensive industry like ours an incentive scheme, based on Work Measurement, is vital. Time Study is used to provide a description of how a standard time for an operation is identified. 'Predetermined Motion Time System' are now the normal method for work measurement: their origins and characteristics are discussed.

Balancing

When the production of a garment is broken down in the interests of efficiency the work of the specialists must be co-ordinated, in order that they produce garments at the same rate. A buffer of garments between the specialist operations (work in process) helps to overcome short-term problems. Good balancing and small stocks of work in process are the hallmarks of an efficient factory. Detailed worked examples help the reader to understand the principles involved.

Production systems, planning and control

All managers must, and all supervisors, mechanics and the like should, understand the decisions that are taken with respect to the production systems chosen and how the production is planned and controlled. The type of production system in use strongly influences the ease of balancing, whilst the planning and control of production are closely linked to balancing. The first step in any scientific approach to a subject such as 'production systems' is classification and the second characterisation. The third step is to select a system which suits the product range being made, the workforce, the capital available and the local resources for construction and maintenance. Too often the choice is based on a desire to be 'up-to-date' and the pressures exerted by salesmen.

Total quality control, from design to despatch

The quality of a garment must be defined before it can be made and the acceptable limits by which it can depart from the perfect muct be agreed. It can be checked during production by looking at a representative *sample*, in order to identify and eliminate causes of poor work before too many defective garments are made.

Each part of the production process plays its part in achieving the result, starting in the design room or even before that in market research. The quality control department is merely there to provide a service which helps the other departments produce good clothes. ISO 9000 (formerly BS 5750 in the UK) provides the basis for the quality system in clothing factories; its origin and purpose are discussed.

Production and people

The ability to persuade people to work in the best interests of the company is the most important that a supervisor or manager can possess. It is a practical skill and one with which theory can provide the least help. Nevertheless there are some ideas that have been shown to work in practice and some background knowledge, which makes it easier to understand why people behave in the way that they do. These are set out here, together with some ideas for exercises, for these are skills which must be learned by doing.

Training

A supervisor or manager without training skills is incompletely equipped. Most will have experienced the poor instructor at one time or another yet few take the trouble to find out how people learn and how they can best be taught. There can be few skills which make such an important contribution to efficiency but which are so widely misunderstood.

Charting and layouts

Any major improvement in productivity will require some changes in layout. These are best shown on charts. Supervisors can often make helpful comments if they are consulted and will usually respond by making a greater effort to make the new layout work. Of course, if their contribution is to be effective, they must understand the principles which guide management when they select a new system.

Using this book

The approach of the student to the book will be governed by the advice of the teaching staff; that of the manager or specialist by the discipline in which he or she was originally trained. Supervisors need guidance. Most have come from the ranks of the sewing, pressing and cutting operatives. They have highly developed practical skills and an instinctive feeling for the way that the work force will react to a proposal. Few will have excelled at academic subjects at school and they probably did not like it very much. A small proportion will have technical qualifications and be strong on theory but lack experience, especially in managing people. Any supervisor from the first group who is reading this book has taken the first step in bridging the gap. Those from the latter are advised to remember that the bare bones of theory, as are set out in the following pages, need to be fleshed out by exposure to the real world of manu-facturing. Nothing is simple except to the partly trained!

1

The Sewing Room Supervisor

Introduction

Why the sewing room?

Most of the supervisors in a clothing factory are in the sewing room. Often they will have received less formal training than those in other departments such as the cutting room. Examples are chosen from the sewing room in order to make points in practical terms.

The supervisor's job

The first step is to see how the supervisors spend their working days and then to see if their priorities are right. Balancing would normally be considered to be the main area in which supervisors can influence productivity. Planning ahead is the keynote. The scheduling of work forms the next most important category. Quality control by the operatives is the way to achieve low quality costs and the supervisor's role is to detect poor work quickly and then to take steps to correct the cause. The specialist staff are there merely to assist in this.

The operatives on the line are the means by which the supervisor gets results. An up-to-date inventory of their skills, together with a determined effort to improve upon them, can do a great deal for section efficiency.

The clerical aspects of a supervisor's work cannot be neglected and it is also important for management to recognise that the effectiveness of supervisors will owe a great deal to their relations with their operatives. These can only be good if the supervisor works to keep them that way.

Supervisory duties

The exact nature of the supervisor's job will vary from factory to factory but an example is provided so that a manager can construct a list appropriate to his or her unit. It helps to let people know exactly what you expect of them. A list prepared by a manager and one prepared by a supervisor will often differ widely.

Factory routines

A good factory routine provides a solid basis for achievement and goes a long way towards eliminating crises. Perhaps the most important aspect is the way that it ensures that regular contact occurs between the manager and all supervisors and that they are prepared for that contact in advance. Good communications are unlikely to occur without it. Regular 'objective' and 'attainment' sessions, on a three-monthly basis, are recommended.

Supervisor's check list

A summary of duties in this form is a good way of establishing what the manager expects in the way of routine for the supervisors. It can be very useful for new supervisors.

> GOOD SUPERVISORS AIM FOR
> THE GREATEST OUTPUT
> AT THE AGREED QUALITY
> FOR THE LEAST COST

The supervisor's job

Breakdown of responsibility

It is useful, as an exercise for supervisors, for them to keep a check on how they spend their days. Students can learn a lot by working with supervisors and then comparing the proportion of the time that each spends on the activities listed. This can then be compared privately with their effectiveness as defined by the production manager, together with indicators such as section efficiency, defects per 1000 standard minutes and absenteeism.

Analysis of Supervision	Hours/week	% time
Production – balancing and delivery Quality Operative Skills – versatility training – initial training Clerical including bonus checking Welfare and other activities Sewing		

Priorities

The proportion of the supervisor's time which is devoted to each activity will depend upon many things, of which the two most important are the company production policy and the personality of the supervisor concerned. In most cases, however, the bulk of a supervisor's time *should* be spent in overcoming or avoiding problems directly related to production and particularly in balancing the output of her team. The supervisor should be motivated to allocate time according to the needs of the job.

> AVOID EMERGENCIES

Balancing

Senior management will select the production system, the degree of sectionalised working and the amount of work in process permitted. These in turn will influence the time that a supervisor should spend in ensuring that the line is and will stay in balance. Nevertheless it is likely that effective supervisors will spend more than half their time in this activity. Much can be achieved by visual balancing but it is essential that written checks are carried out too. It is important that these are done at the agreed times, since the 'supervisor's balance sheet' is a useful document for management only if they can rely on the accuracy of the information. Over-frequent checks will interfere with the supervisor's other work and will lead to fictional accounts. One purpose of the regular check is to provide an opportunity for the supervisor to speak with every operative on the line. Capacity checks can also play a major part in improving individual ouput and also in balancing routine.

Computerised balancing requires the same level of understanding of the balancing process but reduces the chore of regular checks.

Delivery

A production schedule is vital if deliveries are to be made on time. A simple wall chart on which production days are shown will often be adequate to mark the progress of orders and to indicate deadines. On the shop floor the first and last bundles in an order should be noted by the supervisor and reported daily as a check on progress. Supervisors should be told when to expect work and the date by which the last bundle must be completed, in order that the delivery date can be achieved. A written schedule for each week should be issued in advance.

$$\boxed{\text{Throughput time}} = \boxed{\begin{array}{l}\text{Total time that}\\\text{work is in progress}\\\text{in each section from}\\\text{cutting to despatch}\end{array}} + \boxed{\begin{array}{l}\text{Delay time between}\\\text{each section}\end{array}}$$

Priority bundles require colour coding and should be reported separately.

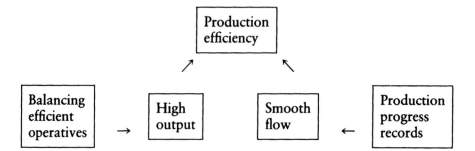

Quality

The achievement of *consistent quality* at the *required level* should be the supervisor's aim. Records of rework, repairs and rejects enable the manager and supervisor to monitor this activity and to take corrective action *before* too much defective work has been produced. The information must be presented simply in such a way that it can be easily analysed. Complicated mathematics are counter-productive in this field although long-term monitoring of trends may be treated in a more sophisticated way. It must be read and used on a regular basis rather than whenever a quality drive is on. It must be *seen* to be used. Anticipation of defects by noting likely causes has also a part to play.

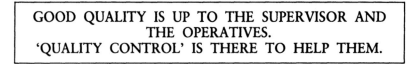

GOOD QUALITY IS UP TO THE SUPERVISOR AND
THE OPERATIVES.
'QUALITY CONTROL' IS THERE TO HELP THEM.

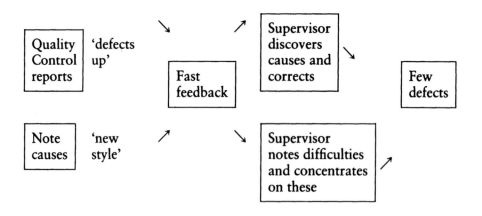

Operative skills

Supervisors are as good as the operatives who work for them. Their achievement in balancing can only be as good as their knowledge of the skill inventory, with plans for increasing the operator performance on normal tasks and for encouraging versatility. It is the mark of the effective supervisor, who should be encouraged to regard it as a source of pride. The initial labour allocation for a section to cope with a style will be agreed with management but the supervisor should be alert to changes in conditions and to possible improvements in the efficiency of the section. Suggestions for change should come from the supervisor upwards and should preferably be for improvements in section efficiency – more garments from fewer people.

Method analysis is useful when operatives appear to be producing less than would be expected from their efforts. Once defective methods have been identified then retraining is possible. The supervisor must anticipate labour turnover and plan for replacements. Equally vital is the need to make new operatives feel at home and to bring them (with help from the trainers) to high efficiency as soon as posisble.

Training

The demand for good training comes naturally from the desire of a supervisor to improve the efficiency of the section. A separate training section can be useful in training new starters and retraining operators to correct their methods or to acquire new skills. 'On the job' instructors may be available to assist the supervisor in overcoming training problems on the production line.

If supervisors do not agree with the methods of the training specialists they must *never* say so to trainees but discuss the matter honestly and privately with the specialists themselves. In this way the respect of the trainee for both supervisor and instructor can be maintained. Even skilled operatives can be improved with tactful coaching and although the co-operation of the specialists should always be sought, the final responsibility for the training of operatives rests with the supervisor.

Clerical

Very few people like paper-work and since it is, of itself, nonproductive, we must keep it to a minimum. But if it is to be done it is better that it is well done. Inaccurate checks, carried out at the wrong times, are harmful.

For example, where there is a daily coupon sheet, it must be verified and initialed by the supervisor, before it is handed into the payroll office. The next day, when it is returned with the performance and the bonus calculated, the supervisor should note the performance recorded and comment on any significant change to the operative. The supervisor should make sure that each operative understands how the bonus is calculated and discuss any points of disagreement, passing them on if appropriate. If at all possible, queries should be answered the same day.

Welfare and other activities

Supervisors should be encouraged to regard the welfare of operatives as *their* responsibility. After all, the supervisor knows them best and by helping them with their problems, can establish a good working relationship. Nevertheless, the personnel officer and factory nurse as useful aides and not as rivals. Their assistance should be sought with anything that is time-consuming.

Up to 10 per cent of a supervisor's time may usefully be spent talking with operatives on matters not strictly related to production. Studies have shown that this is essential for the friendly co-operation which marks a successful section.

Sample of a list of supervisory duties

Production

Planning
- Planning the allocation of the operatives within the section, in order to balance throughput.
- Ensuring that cut work, garments from another section, thread and trimmings are ordered, with adequate notice and checks on delivery.
- Recommending people for transfer to other tasks or asking for additional operatives, in order to maintain manning levels.
- Preparing a chart showing the potential output of each of the operatives for various jobs ('skills inventory').

Quality
- Checking that work is produced within quality tolerances.
- Inspecting some of the work passed by the examiners, correcting them as necessary, and informing the Quality Manager of major problems.
- Reporting excessive numbers of cloth defects and poor quality from other parts of the factory.

Operatives

Recruitment and discharge
- Asking for labour when the need is known, so that replacement can be planned.
- Enquiring as to the reasons for resignations and reporting the facts.

Induction
- Giving information to trainees on the garments made and how they are manufactured.
- Introducing new employees to the section, factory facilities and rules.
- Ensuring that new starters know the safety rules and obey them.

Training
- Noting the training needs of the operatives. One or more skills for ordinary operatives must be agreed with management on the skills inventory.
- Giving instruction, as required, and reporting on the progress made.
- Controlling the trainees on the line.
- Liaising with the Training Centre on trainees destined for the line.

Utilisation
- Moving operatives about, in order to maintain the section at its highest efficiency.
- Discussing with management, on a daily basis, the movement of people to and from the section in order to cope with absenteeism.

Discipline
- Working within the factory disciplinary procedures.
- Dealing with lateness, absenteeism and over-extended breaks.
- Making sure that the members of the section are familiar with the company rules and seeing that these are obeyed.
- Making recommendation to management on suspension and discharge.

Safety
- Understanding the applications of the Factories Act.
- Allowing only safe working practices.
- Checking that all machinery in the section is in safe working order or has been checked by a competent person.
- Sending injured people to the First Aid Assistant.
- Advising management when to contact the Fire Brigade or the Hospital.

Labour relations
- Dealing with the personal problems of the section, as far as possible, and passing on to management only those where help is required.
- Reporting all possible causes of industrial unrest.
- Passing on to the responsible person any official union complaints.

Methods

Study
- Making recommendations for improved methods and layouts.
- Checking that standard practices produce garments which are up to the required standard of quality.
- Ensuring that the standard methods, tools, machinery and layouts are used.
- Requesting reviews of unsatisfactory practices or time standards.
- Giving instruction to the operatives on the standard practices,

especially operating methods.
- Investigating and reporting on the reasons for poor quality or volume of output.

Money

Wages
- Handling queries about wages and bonuses, but reporting to the Wages Office if help is needed to resolve the problem.
- Collecting and delivering coupon sheets and weekly pay sheets.
- Checking and completing coupon sheets.
- Approving and identifying causes of off-standard time.
- Ensuring that operatives book off and on standard at the correct time.

Costs
- Correcting off-standard conditions where possible.
- Tackling causes of poor quality in the garments made, in order to keep the number of seconds and rejects to a minimum. This applies to labour as well as machines.
- In a similar way, tackling the causes of stoppages, in order to keep these as few as possible.
- Ensuring that the section is kept 'on standard' as much as possible.

Factory routine

Purpose

Most work study engineers would agree that a skilled operative can be recognised by smooth rhythmic action, with no unnecessary movement. Similarly, a skilled manager can be recognised by a factory where things run smoothly with a consistent pace and the minimum of emergencies.

The fewer the emergencies the more management time there is available to cope with them and to plan the prevention of re-occurrences. The answer lies not in rules but in a clear understanding by everyone of what they have to do and when, of the limits of their responsibility, of other. peoples' responsibilities and the criteria by which performance is judged.

Planning

The main difference between the manager's and the supervisor's daily work-load is in the proportion of time allocated to planning and in the interpretation of factual data to monitor actual production against plans, in order to take corrective action:

The most important aspect is production planning, to ensure that each line is kept supplied with work and that, subject to cloth availability, etc. each line produces garments of the same sort for as long a run as possible.

With the minimum of relearning to do, both operatives and supervisors perform better so that a higher volume and more consistent quality result.

Good planning ensures that materials, cut-work and trimmings are ready in advance and that where more than one section is involved, adequate time is allowed for a garment to go through the first line before it is required on the second in order that delivery dates are met. Shortages of specialised machinery or labour with special skills should also be anticipated.

Good planning is the basis of an effective factory routine.

Management information

This serves two purposes: it permits the manager to monitor actual performance, so that corrective action can be taken; and it permits agreement on targets with subordinates, so that their effectiveness can be judged impartially.

We all do better if we have a target for our performance. Ratios such as section efficiency can be a subject of pride for a good supervisor. It is best to concentrate on the positive aspects of performance as far as possible, since most people perform better when they are trying to live up to high expectations.

Weekly meetings

Weekly section performance, particularly with respect to off-standard time, are usually a better guide to trends than daily performances. However, these are best considered for each supervisor in turn after the daily meeting. The weekly meeting should be devoted to factory performance under its various headings and the contribution that can be made by each supervisor or head of a service unit to improvement.

Example
Time off standard is high overall and particularly in Jean's and Betty's sections. Furthermore they may point out that this is due to excessive 'machine breakdown'. The problem can then be left to Jean, Betty and the chief mechanic to investigate so that they can report back at the next meeting.

Weekly meetings should take place in factory time, where possible, and should be limited to half an hour or so.

After hours meetings

'Off the job' training is best confined to an introduction to techniques which can then be practised 'on the job'. Where it is impractical to conduct these in factory time it is usually best to follow them with a social evening at factory expense rather than merely to pay overtime. Most supervisors have families to look after and a training session at 7.30

pm followed by a social evening is normally much preferred to a session immediately after working hours.

After hours meetings should not, in general, take place more often than once a month.

Key Result Areas

Some factories run on a series of 'blitzes'. For example, an order is lost because of poor quality. As a result everyone concentrates upon 'quality improvement' to the exclusion of all else, until the next crisis. Periodic meetings (usually quarterly) between the manager and each supervisor are better. Then the particular needs (Key Result Areas) of the supervisor's section can be identified and objectives set to meet them. Where possible these objectives should have quantified targets and a date by which they should be completed.

If the 'Key Result Area' is quality, then the supervisor may agree to reduce the rejects from final examination to 15 per cent, by the end of the quarter. Sometimes an individual 'KRA' may lie outside of normal work and this gives a form of controlled flexibility to the job description. For example, a supervisor may agree to work for an hour a day with the mechanic in designing work aids, in addition to normal duties.

It is seldom sensible to agree more than four objectives to be completed within a quarter.

Supervisor training needs

List of supervisory duties

Go through the example provided in this chapter. Amend it to correspond with the conditions in your factory. Are there any other activities which concern supervisors and have not been covered?

Priorities

- How well is each duty being done at present?
- How big a part do supervisors play in controlling it?
- How much difference does it make to the profitability of the factory?

From these questions a few key result areas will emerge. From these it will be necessary to select those which can be tackled with a fair chance of success, in order to provide confidence for further work.

What can be done?

- What are the options for overcoming the difficulty?
- How big a part can training play?
- What needs to be done before training can start?

Feedback

- How do you know if a function is done properly?
- Can the information be quantified?
- Can better control information be provided at an economic cost?
- Who needs to receive the control information?
- How will the supervisors receive it?

Training programme

What? Where? When? Why? How? Who? *Will the benefit outweigh the cost?*

Supervisor's check list

(a) Start up

1. *Manning*	– visual check of section, note absentees, allocate floaters.
	– discuss with management if necessary.
2. *Daily book*	– check coupon sheets.
	– enter totals in book.
	– 'post' coupon sheets.

(b) Regular checks

1. *Hourly checks*	– balancing sheet.
	– work in process.
	– plan ahead.
	– more operators if required.
2. *Quality checks*	– at passing, key operation, learners.
	– discuss with operators concerned.

(c) Once a day

1. *Manager's rounds*	– show book.
	– discuss yesterday's output and today's plans.
2. *Capacity checks*	– at least two operators per day.
	– concentrate on weak lines.
	– combine with method and quality check.
3. *Visit trainees*	– in training centre.
	– in section.
4. *General tidiness*	– work places, void coupons to boxes, etc.
	– gangways–beware of the danger of obstructions.

5.	*Machines*	– look for signs of troubles developing. – outstanding repairs from previous day. – condition of spare machine(s).
6.	*Time-keeping*	– late coming. – inaccurate booking of off-standard time. – meal breaks.
7.	*Coupon sheets*	– collect finished sheets, examine and distribute. – re-collect and return to office.

(d) Close down

| 1. | *Manning* | – probable absentees for next day.
– operatives who are feeling unwell. |
| 2. | *Machines* | – all switched off at end of day. |

(e) Weekly

1.	*Bonus and hours*	– recorded accurately, agreed by operator.
2.	*Performance*	– up or down. – comparison with capacity checks.
3.	*Planning*	– work coming on to section. – new styles or cloths. – manning required. – targets.
4.	*Supervisors' sections*	– off-standard time and reasons. – quality standards. – total output and efficiencies.
5.	*Special efforts*	– aspect of supervision to receive special attention in the coming week. – effect of special effort in previous week.

Key points

1.	*Know*	what is happening in your section.
2.	*Anticipate*	what will happen next.
3.	*Decide*	what you will do about it.
4.	*Routine.*	Get things done with minimum effort and nothing missed.

2

How Output is Lost

Introduction

Cutting the cost for each garment

The costs of production can be divided into two main categories: those that change little with output ('overheads') and those which vary almost in proportion to it ('direct costs'). The cost of the overheads which is allocated to each garment can best be reduced by keeping every production workplace busy. The direct costs can be kept down by greater efficiency. Sewing room supervisors cannot do much to control the cost of cloth but they can greatly reduce the cost of the labour. The areas of potential savings are threefold:

- higher occupancy of work stations;
- greater output per person 'on standard';
- a minimum of time spent 'off standard'.

An operative is said to be 'on standard' when doing the job for which he or she is trained and equipped. If operatives are on an incentive scheme they should be earning bonus in the standard manner. 'Off standard' covers all of the rest of the working time, exclusive of official breaks. The time spent on each is usually shown on the individual pay card and, for the factory or section, on the management information sheets.

Calculating how much output is lost

First it is necessary to calculate how much work could be done if every worker were fully employed at a standard performance. This gives the number of standard hours of work which could be produced. Then the reasons why workers may be unoccupied or ineffective are considered.

Next the causes of lost efficiency when 'on standard' are examined and the losses estimated from poor methods and/or operative performance.

Finally the losses from time 'off standard' are listed: machine delays; unmeasured work; repairs and rejects; waiting time; balancing; work study and samples.

It will be seen that most factories operate at about half their potential.

Standard work content

The exact nature of standard work content is described in Chapter 4. It reflects the output of a well trained and motivated operative, using the right equipment and working to the agreed quality level. In part it is determined by the garment design and in part by the level of workplace engineering in the factory. The standard work content of an order is the time which would be taken by the labour force, if they were all working at a standard rate for all of the time. In some cases it may include the budgeted time for the hourly paid direct labour.

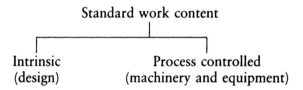

Standard work content

Intrinsic
(design)

Process controlled
(machinery and equipment)

Supervisors are most likely to be able to help to reduce the standard work content by making suggestions with respect to work aids and so reducing the process controlled part.

Excess work content

Excess work content is also of two sorts: policy excess and managerial excess. The first is more to do with the management style of the factory and is concerned with planned throughput time, the frequency of style change and the permitted amount of work in process. All of these are related to the marketing and financial strategy. Managerial excess, on the other hand, is very much in the supervisors' field and covers such items as time spent by operatives doing jobs which are not theirs, because of balancing problems. An important aspect is the wasted work when a garment is badly made, so that it has to be unpicked and remade.

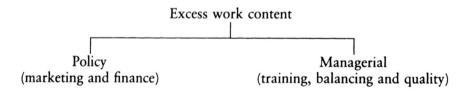

Excess work content

Policy
(marketing and finance)

Managerial
(training, balancing and quality)

Work content

The costs of production

A garment factory is a place where cloth and trimmings are turned into garments by people and machines. Some of the costs are called 'overheads' and do not vary much with the output which comes out. These are the costs of the building(s), machines and fixtures; management and supervisory staff and also ancillary workers like the examiners and cleaners. Other costs are more easily identified with output and for that reason we call them the 'direct' costs.

Potential production

For any unit there will be a limit to the number of direct operatives that can be accommodated efficiently. Indeed, the author recalls on assignment where the output was increased by reducing the number of machinists employed! In Britain it is usual to work only five days a week for one shift. Supervision has control only over the output for the accepted working week. Except in the cutting room, the supervisors have little effect on the material and trimmings costs. Their main impact comes in the way that they use the workplaces allotted to them. Each workplace can be considered to have a potential for production of the hours which go to make up the working week.

Manufacturing time

The actual time to produce a garment in a factory can be considered in two parts: the *standard* and the *excess*. The reason for recognising these separately is that their level is determined by different people, so that their reduction and control must be achieved in different ways. The 'standard time' represents the number of working hours (or minutes) required under standard conditions to produce the garment. It is usual to refer to this as the 'standard work content' or, less correctly, as the 'work content'.

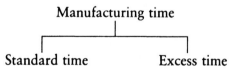

Intrinsic and process controlled work content

Standard work content = Intrinsic work content + Process controlled work content

Intrinsic work content depends upon:

● number and shape of cut parts;

- number and nature of seams;
- decorative features;
- cloth and trimmings selection;
- stitches per inch;
- thread changes during and between bundles;
- check matching;
- basting and underpressing;
- hand work;
- quality standards.

Process controlled work content depends upon:

- working conditions – lighting and comfort;
- degree of job fragmentation – sectionalisation;
- machinery – suitablity, speed and attachments;
- work aids – shelves, pick-up devices, etc.
- automatic machinery – related to the scale of production, sectionalisation, availability of suitable maintenance staff and capital;
- special processes – fusing, etc.

Whilst the intrinsic work content depends upon the market requirements it may be reduced by suitable 'garment engineering' and this subject is discussed later under 'Quality'. The process controlled work content can be reduced by investing in new machinery but this must always be considered in the light of possible savings and the probable length of time for which the new machinery will be of use.

Policy and managerial excess

Excess work content = Actual making time – Standard work content
= Policy excess + Managerial excess

$$\frac{\text{Excess work content}}{\text{Standard work content}} \times 100 = \% \text{ Excess}$$

Policy excess depends upon:

- throughput time – limits on work in process;
- rate of style change – retraining, balancing changes, etc.
- rate of fabric change – handling changes, process changes;
- size of unit – possiblity of sectionalisation;
- percentage of made to measure.

Managerial excess can be evaluated by considering items which management and supervision can affect:

- labour turnover – balancing upsets and training costs;

- operative training efficiency – average time to 75 BSI (British Standard Institute), etc.
- absenteeism – balancing upsets and quality problems;
- degree of part-time working – investment costs per hour are higher;
- ratio of supervisors' – to direct labour hours;
- operative utilisation – work off standard may lower motivation and lead to failure to use special equipment;
- operative efficiency – the ultimate requirement;
- operative performance – with low labour turnover this should approach 100 BSI.

Efficiency

If we can measure work in the currency of the standard minute, then we have an absolute measure of output, which does not change for a given factory with a given set of machinery and equipment. By comparing this with the potential, that is the time attended, we can measure the level of efficiency. (The term can equally well be applied to a section or an operative, but operative efficiency should not be confused with operative performance: see also Chapter 4).

$$\text{Efficiency} = \frac{\text{Standard minutes earned}}{\text{Actual minutes attended}}$$

Utilisation

Good supervisors keep people at their proper jobs as much as possible. On any other they will probably lack the necessary skill and equipment and will probably not be on incentive. Naturally they will produce less than usual.

$$\text{Operative utilisation} = \frac{\text{Minutes on standard}}{\text{Minutes attended}}$$

Time spent 'off standard' may be totally unproductive, as when an operative is waiting for a machine to be repaired and there is no other suitable work.

Operative performance

Even when an operative is on standard the output will depend upon the skill and effort and the level of output will depend upon the performance.

$$\text{Operative performance} = \frac{\text{SM earned on standard}}{\text{Minutes spent on standard}}$$

Improving profitability

Overhead recovery

Every workplace bears its share of the overheads. The first step in making it pay its way is to ensure that 'there is a bottom on every stool' and that bottom should belong to a skilled operative. Empty workplaces can be caused by a variety of things of which the chief are listed.

Labour turnover
Skilled labour is a vital asset to any company; its replacement is an expensive necessity, which should be kept to a minimum.

Operator training
The cost of labour turnover and the necessary training of new recruits can be minimised by effective instruction. Beginners on lines cause balancing and quality problems and so they are usually given their initial instruction off the job. The better the instruction, the faster the throughput and the lower the cost of the training centre.

Replacement planning
Whilst operatives are brought up to the minimum standard off the job there may be a empty workplace in the section, which is not paying its way. If warning can be given of the need for replacement skills this can be avoided. Fast training helps too.

Absenteeism
An absent operative not only represents a loss of hours available for productive work but is a cause of line imbalance.

Part-time working
As machines increase in cost so the economics of employing part-timers become even more suspect. A happy working atmosphere makes it easier to recruit and to retain labour and so helps to reduce the dependence on part-timers.

Operative efficiency

A manned workplace may still produce less than it should. This can only be because it is not being used properly or because the operative is not working hard enough. Motivation is covered in a later chapter but it is worthwhile to note that good supervisors seem to get more work out of their teams than poor ones. Inefficient use has two main causes: poor methods and 'off standard work'.

Poor methods

Improving methods
There is always a better way. Operatives and supervisors can always help with this. Most Work Study Officers spend too much time on Work Measurement.

Operative performance
The use of non-standard methods can account for substantial losses of output. Their identification and improvement by retraining is a key area for production management. The operative is not likely to be properly motivated unless there is a good incentive scheme which is clearly understood. The non-financial incentives are important too. Style change without proper retraining is another source of loss.

'Off standard work'

In most clothing factories most machinists are on some form of incentive payment whilst they are doing the job for which they are trained and equipped. They are then said to be 'on standard'. If they come off incentive or 'off standard' they will have no financial incentive to work hard. Even if work is found which they are able to tackle their output will probably halve.

In most companies provision is made on the payroll software for the recording of the proportion of time spent off and on standard and for the off standard time to be analysed.

This analysis is intended to highlight the causes of off standard time, which can be investigated further if the proportions are unusually high. The exact categorisation varies but the principal categories are discussed below.

Machine delay
Some off standard time due to breakdowns is inevitable, especially as specialised machinery and purpose-built workplaces become more important. However, it can be kept to a minimum if supervisors and operatives are taught the correct way in which to rectify minor faults and to avoid trouble by using the machine correctly; and if there are spare machines, routine maintenance and – most important of all – a well trained and adequately manned engineering section.

Unmeasured work
Adequate liaison at the manning stage and the use of garment synthetics should reduce this to a minimum. In many factories temporary rates can be installed based entirely on garment synthetics, and these can eliminate this category entirely.

Repairs and rejects
Repairs are commonly considered to double the labour cost of a garment because of the time taken in identification, unpicking and remaking, together with the problems of the subsequent matching of repaired garments to bundles.

Waiting time
This term is normally applied to time spent waiting for trimmings or work from another section. The supervisor may have little control over it.

Balancing
Because different workplaces will have different output rates the section will inevitably move out of balance. Off standard time as listed above will also contribute. High work in process stocks smooth out the flow at the cost of increased overheads.

Training
Operatives will need retraining on the line, because of style change or to get rid of poor methods. Training in versatility is also important. Training can be done in short periods towards the end of the day as an aid to balancing.

Work study
If operatives are asked to try out new methods they will usually clock off standard. Wherever possible, new methods should be proved by the instructors and supervisors first.

Samples
Samples should be made on the line wherever possible. They cause upsets in production but are often the only way to discover the snags.

Calculating how much output is lost

Set out below is an example with the facts drawn from a typical British company. Readers are advised to substitute figures from their own unit and to redo the calculation. The data which is not available from records should be obtained from short sample studies. The results are of help in emphasising key areas in which improvements can be made. This is particularly true of the 'off standard' categories, where supervisors can make the most impact. For ease of calculation some insignificant approximations have been made.

There are 100 work stations, of which some may be set aside for 'off the job' training. Each year has 48 weeks, each of which has 40 working hours.
   The potential performance from trained operatives on the factory floor is taken as 100.

Labour turnover is 24 per cent per annum and 1 per cent of the workplaces are vacant whilst leavers are replaced.

'Off the job' training occurs in the area designated as the 'Training Centre', where the instructors operate. Work must be brought to it and returned to the production lines by the trainees. Only some of their output is useful. The average time taken to reach the leaving performance of 75 is 20 weeks. The average useful output per trainee is 25.

From the Training Centre operatives move on to the factory floor, where their learning is under the control of the supervisors. This is considered to have finished when they achieve a stable performance of 100 or more for a week. On average this, too, takes about 20 weeks. During this period the average performance is 85.

Absenteeism	10%	Machine delay idle	1%
Part-timers (4 hours/day)	10%	other work	4%
Methods 90% effective		Unmeasured work	20%
Average factory		Others' repairs	2%
performance	90*	Waiting time	1%
Repairs returned to		Balancing	5%
operative	10%	Work study	1%
Rejects	2%		

* For work done 'on standard'.

	Potential (standard hours/week)
Without lost output	4,000
Lost due to labour turnover @ 24% p.a.	

At Training Centre = ('off the job')

$$100 \times \frac{24}{100} \times \frac{20}{48} \times 40\left[\frac{(100-25)}{100} = 0.75\right]$$

'On the job' training =

$$100 \times \frac{24}{100} \times \frac{20}{48} \times 40\left[\frac{(100-85)}{100} = 0.15\right]$$

Therefore total loss in training = $100 \times \frac{24}{100} \times \frac{20}{48} \times 40[0.9] =$ 360

Loss due to delay in recruitment	40
Total	400
Potential remaining	3,600

Absenteeism @ 10%

$$3,600 \times \frac{(100-10)}{100}$$
3,240

Part timers @ 10% on a 4-hour day

Lost output is $3,240 \times \frac{10}{100} \times \frac{4}{8} = 162$
3,078

Poor methods (90% effective)

$$3{,}078 \times \frac{(100 - 90)}{100} \hspace{4cm} 2{,}770$$

Poor performance by 'trained' operatives

Average performance 90% of potential: $2{,}770 \times \dfrac{90}{100}$ $\hspace{2cm}$ 2,493

'Off standard' work
This represents a loss of potential even when the operative is working, since there is no incentive for extra effort.

Machine delay @ 1% idle and 4% @ 50 performance

$$\text{Lost output is } 1\% + 4\% \times \frac{(90 - 50)}{100} = \hspace{1cm} 2.6\%$$

Unmeasured work @ 20% @ 70 performance

$$\text{Lost output is } 20\% \times \frac{(90 - 70)}{100} = \hspace{1cm} 4.0\%$$

Other repairs @ 2%
    Lost output $\hspace{4cm}$ 2.0%
Waiting time @ 1%
    Lost output $\hspace{4cm}$ 1.0%
Balancing @ 5% @ 50 performance

$$\text{Lost output is } 5\% \times \frac{(90 - 50)}{100} = \hspace{1cm} 2.0\%$$

Work Study @ 1% @ 50 performance

$$\text{Lost output is } 1\% \times \frac{(90 - 50)}{100} = \hspace{1cm} 0.4\%$$

Samples are negligible

Total $\hspace{5cm}$ 12.0%

$$2{,}493 \times \frac{(100 - 12)}{100} \hspace{4cm} 2{,}194$$

Poor quality
Own repairs @ 10% with additional work @ 50%

$$\text{Lost output is } 10\% \times \frac{50}{100} = \hspace{1cm} 5.0\%$$

Rejects @ 2% $\hspace{5cm}$ 2.0%
Total $\hspace{5.5cm}$ 7.0%

$$2{,}194 \times \frac{(100 - 7)}{100} \hspace{4cm} 2{,}040$$

$$\therefore \text{ Lost output is } \frac{(4{,}000 - 2{,}040)}{4{,}000} = \frac{1{,}960}{4{,}000} \text{ or } 49\%$$

3
Basic Method Study

Introduction

What is Work Study?

Over the years the term has come to cover a wide range of techniques and there is a great deal of overlap with other disciplines such as 'organisation and methods' and 'operation research'. The basic tools are method study and work measurement.

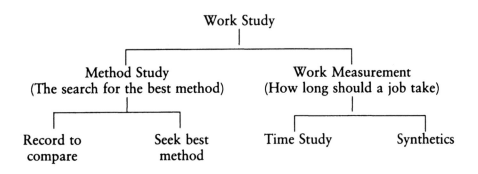

The most important aspect is that it tries to substitute fact for opinion and to promote an ordered and logical approach to problems, particularly problems of production. Like any other trade it has developed its own jargon and mystique which present a barrier to the understanding of its basic principles. The reader should ignore this and remember that much of the subject is applied commonsense. Indeed, some of the refinements are considered by some to have positive disadvantages. Ralph Presgrave, commenting on the dubious 'law' of motion time, is particularly scathing and goes on to say:

'Further to such laws we have thousands of examples of scientific mummery in the shape of formulas, which apparently have no other purpose than to satisfy an inner urge on the part of the formulator, or to dazzle the reader.' *The Dynamics of Time Study.*

Why do we use Method Study?

(1)   Different operatives will develop different ways of doing a job. Not all can be right.
(2)   Some ways of working may have been developed because they were easier to learn or the operative had a special skill.
(3)   The systematic recording of methods is essential for Work Measurement and helps when we wish to compare different approaches.
(4)   The identification of the best method is a skill, learned by practice, like all other skills. It is not uncommon for a good consultant to walk around a factory and to stop at an inefficient operation without any of the conscious selection which is preached in this text. But by carefully examining methods in a critical way, we gradually acquire the skill to identify bad ones and to suggest better ones.
(5)   One argument for a specialist practitioner is that better methods can sometimes only come from a factory-wide change. However, supervisors and managers, especially managers, must try to keep up to date on the latest work aids. Then they have an advantage over the operative when seeking 'the better way'. The operative has to adapt his or her method to suit the workplace and garment presentation provided by management. Some work aids can be developed by Method Study.

> BETTER METHODS MEAN MORE PRODUCTIVITY.
> MORE PRODUCTIVITY MEANS MORE PROSPERITY

To get more garments out of a factory using the same number of people we can:

*   work longer hours;
*   work harder;
*   use better methods.

Which would you prefer, as an operative?

Why do we use Work Measurement?

In the nineteenth century a worker might contract to sew the side seams on skirts at 2d per skirt. If the fabric were light she might be able to do ten an hour. If it were heavy this might be cut to seven.

In a similar way the time taken to do the job could depend upon a number of factors like the length of the skirt, the number of stitches per inch and the presence of flounces around the hem.

Work Measurement provides a fair way of estimating the time that it should take to do a job, given the right skills, a plentiful work supply and the proper equipment. Nowadays we use the 'standard minute' as a tool for balancing, production control and the estimation of efficiency. It is important in accurate pricing and, of course, in modern incentive schemes. It is a measure of the work content of a garment as the yard or metre is of the cloth.

Method Study and Work Measurement

Work Measurement *must be fair* and it is essential that the conditions of the work when studied are set out clearly. So, we record what the workplace was like, the size and style of the garments, the stitches per inch and other quality standards. We also record, as best we can, the method used. A trap set by the wily operative for the inexperienced Work Study practitioner is to use an inefficient method when being studied! Method improvements can occur during the production life of a style. Better machines can be installed and new work aids devised. All of these alter the true standard time.

All practitioners make mistakes, from time to time, in setting rates. Performances which are unusually high or low should always be investigated but it is foolish indeed, having discovered slack rates, to adjust the method and retime – just as foolish as it is for the shop steward to be forever challenging rates, so that the Work Study Officer has to check them. The time spent on Method Study might lead to improvements which would make it possible to pay everybody more or at least to keep jobs secure.

Courtesy

Before making a study the supervisor must be approached, not only to request permission to do the work but because valuable advice might be given as to whom it is best to study and the best time for it. The supervisor may also be able to ensure that the operative is not interrupted during the study. It is always important to explain to the operative the purpose and the nature of the study. Where it is necessary to study leg and foot movements, permission must be sought from the operative. It is preferable to give notice at least a day in advance, especially where photographs and/or video films are to be taken. The effect of floodlights on the section must always be considered and warning must be given of flash, where there are people nearby who are doing dangerous work. Always thank the people concerned for their help afterwards.

Method Study's part in your job

Everybody's concern

Method Study is very much part of the modern clothing factory. The management, supervisors and, in certain cases, the operatives can all make a better contribution to the prosperity of the company if they take an active and well-informed part in the improvement of method. For the engineers, trainers and quality staff it is an essential part of their job. Some of the more important aspects are set out below.

- Recommendations for improved methods and layouts.
- Checks that garments are made according to the approved methods or there is a good reason for the deviation.
- Checks on the effectiveness of the approved methods in producing garments up to the required standard of quality.
- Evaluation of new work aids and machinery with a view to their installation.
- Implementing new methods.

Every member of the management team must be able to understand the services available from the Work Study Department and be able to use the simpler techniques in order to do their own job better.

Examples

If a supervisor can help an operative who has difficulty in making a reasonable bonus, there will be a gain in efficiency and an increase in the respect and gratitude of the operative. Most supervisors are ex-machinists but may have little experience of the job concerned. The supervisor's own way may not be the best one or suitable for that particular operative. Method Study offers help in understanding what is wrong and in putting it right.

(1) An experienced operative finds difficulty in meeting the target, although working hard. The supervisor looks at the complete cycle and notices that the needle becomes unthreaded at the end of the cycle. The supervisor checks through the probable causes and compares the operative's method with the correct sequence. The machine is tried to see if it is working properly. It is noticed that the operative has a bandaged knee and does not appear to be actuating the knee press fully on every cycle.
   The mechanic therefore replaces the knee press with a thumb actuated switch.
(2) A machinist is transferred from the 'briefs' section to 'slips', side-seam operation. She brings her own lockstitch machine with her.

The supervisor is newly promoted from 'bras'. First the supervisor does a detailed Method Study on an experienced machinist, writing down what is seen and notes that the new operative takes six bursts to sew the seam.

A spare instructress therefore comes over to teach the machinist how to let the material flow whilst machining instead of 'sew', 'reposition hands' and 'sew'. The handling for long seams is different from that for short ones.

(3) Several operatives suffer from a fall-off in performance. A quick Method Study shows an unusual number of fumbles on 'pick up ply and position'. The cause is identified as fused edges and the average time for this element is much higher than it should be.

The supervisor tackles the cutting room foreman with the hard evidence and he agrees to see that his staff stop a reoccurrence. He might have treated a less factual complaint less seriously.

These problems and their solutions are taken from an actual supervisor training programme and they are fairly straightforward, as they need to be for the purposes of illustration. However, some supervisors have pioneered major improvements with a little help from the factory Work Study Officer. If properly handled, the most important aspect of supervisor training in Method Study is the increased co-operation between them and the Work Study Officers. Of course, wrongly handled, the reverse can be true.

Sequence of improvement

EAD

The selection of the best method must be done in a systematic way. A suggested sequence is set out below but there is often a lot of backtracking in practice. The list makes sure that nothing important is left out. The mnemonic for this suggests the preposterous slogan 'use your EAD'. At least it is easy to remember.

Examination	Is the operation necessary?
	Are parts best done elsewhere?
	Are the machine and needle right for the job?
	Is the material likely to change?
Analysis	How is the operation best performed?
	What aids can assist?
	What changes in layout will help?
	What effect will these changes have on the previous and subsequent operation?
Discussion and test	with the operative(s) and instructor for their comments and to keep them informed.

to test rival elements.
to give the operative a chance to practise.
with the WSO if there has been no prior involvement.

Examination

This typifies the Work Study approach by getting down to basics. Why bother to improve the method for sewing a seam which can be eliminated or done more cheaply on a different type of machine? It is not uncommon to find an operative who seems to be using the wrong needle only to find that this is the one which copes with the full range of fabrics and saves time on needle changes. The problem then is to decide whether this should continue or whether an allowance should be paid for the needle changes.

Analysis (record what you see and not what you expect)

If we are familiar with a skill we have a model with which we can compare other methods. We may, however, record what we expect to happen and not what actually occurs.

Record the method first in general terms. If time is short, as it usually is, select for detailed examination parts which seem to be likely to offer the greatest savings. Record one part at a time and wait for it to come round again. The more experienced the observer the larger the piece that can be analysed in one chunk but analysis is very exacting work and it is better in the long run to attempt a little at a time.

Wherever possible, look at several people doing the same job but beware of the left-hander and the superskilled. It often happens that the best method is a combination of elements from different people, with improvements from the person doing the study. Since different people work at different rates of effort and skill, 'normalized' or 'basic' times for the elements are vital in order to compare them. Pay especial attention to jobs for which known work aids are available.

Discussion and test

The involvement of the people concerned will not only bring out any weaknesses in the proposed scheme but is a fine way of ensuring their co-operation in making the new method work. New methods mean new rates. It is helpful to check out the proposed method with the Work Study Officer for the flaws in the study and suggestions about the method. It is essential that proper notice is given of the installation, so that a professional work measurement exercise can be carried out.

The professional approach

Work Study practitioners usually follow a standard routine when they do

Method Study. There are, of course, variations on the theme but the basic pattern can be remembered by the mnemonic 'SREDDIM'.

Select work to be studied.
Record from observation of all relevant facts.
Examine critically (with help from your friends).
Develop the best method and workplace.
Define a new method which gives best economic returns.
Install as a standard practice.
Maintain by regular routine checks.

The benefits against the actual and potential costs should be checked at all stages, especially after the 'develop' stage. Costs include those attributable to Work Study, training, quality control, engineers and to the effect of the interruption of the smooth running of a line.

Principles of motion economy

It is always difficult for beginners to decide on the best method. Yet another mnemonic is useful to make sure that nothing is missed. This is 'MISS CHURN'.

M   The extent of a movement should be kept to a *minimum*.
    Finger   Best
    Fingers
    Hand
    Forearm
    Arm
    Body
    Walking about   Worst
I   People come in different shapes and sizes. As far as possible the workplace should be adjusted to the *individual*.
S   The body naturally adjusts to counterbalance any movement of its parts. Ideally one useful movement should be matched by another, so that they are *symmetrical*.
S   Where possible, movements of the arms and of the other parts of the body should occur together. That is, they should be *simultaneous*.
C   Jerky movement is tiring and unproductive. For the best results movements should be *continuous*, except during rest breaks.
H   When we carry out a new job we must think about the order in which we do things, look ahead to see where parts are and concentrate, in order to work within the limits set. With practice, we can do the same job with the minimum of thought and effort. If the tools and parts are always in the same place the method becomes *habitual*. Even feeding yourself would require a great deal of care if your mouth were in a different place each time.

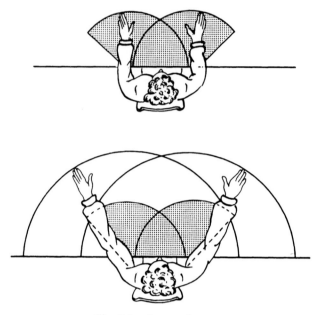

Fig. 3.1   Areas of access.

U Restricted movement is more tiring than *unrestricted* movement. Work aids can often reduce the control that the operative must exert and so make the work less tiring. Edge guides are an example.

R Horses running and fishes swimming do so rhythmically, since this is the economical way. *Rhythmic* movement is natural movement. Nevertheless, some operatives build into their jobs unnecessary movements which, however rhythmic, are wasteful.

N The easiest way is the *natural* way. Sometimes, to the untrained person the easiest way does not seem to be natural but, as training builds up co-ordination, the best way becomes the natural way. Probably crawling seems to be more natural to a toddler than walking.

Figure 3.1 shows how a work surface should be laid out for maximum motion economy, Articles in frequent use should be within the shaded area and all other articles within the unshaded area if possible.

How to record methods

The purpose of these notes

The non-practitioner needs to pay less regard to the conventions of the recording of method studies. Nevertheless, some order is necessary if the best use is to be made of them by the person who makes the notes and others who may wish to read them later. Some understanding of the format and some of the more common abbreviations may help in following studies done by professionals.

Elements

First, see if the job can be broken down into elements, each of which consists of a series of actions which are linked, with a recognisable beginning and an end. If there is an audible signal for these so much the better. Give each element a title and write them down in sequence. It is generally best if the elements take about the same length of time to perform, e.g. 10 seconds, 12 seconds, 6 seconds and 20 seconds. A Work Study practitioner would usually express the time in hundredths of a minute in our industry (centiminutes or CM), e.g. 167 CM which may also be found written as 1.67 minutes.

Where possible, separate machining from non-machining elements, since they have different allowances.

Breakpoints

A breakpoint marks the end of one element and the beginning of another. It is important to have clearly defined breakpoints between elements to make it easier to time them.

Systematic analysis

When first learning Method Study it is best to concentrate on one element at a time, recording, checking and amending until the record is complete. Study – relax – study. It sometimes happens that an unskilled operative will change the method between one cycle and another. It may also be that the method varies for good reason. For example, it is common to have to reverse every other ply because of two-way laying up.

Then, when the study is complete, examine it for discrepancies, and if necessary do a check study. Draw a line between each element, ending with the break point.

Check

When the study is complete check it against the initial record of the work cycle. Finally, take another look at the breakdown into elements, in order to see that they are of about the right length and that different types of work are separated as far as possible. It does no real harm if a very small piece of non-machining work is included with what is mainly a sewing cycle if it makes sense on other counts. For example, 'pick up and position label' may take only 0.05 CM and form part of the 'first sew', which is 0.18 CM if it does not fit easily into the previous element.

Records

Three types of sheet are common. The choice of form depends to some extent on the type of study and to some on the purpose for which it is required. The simple analysis sheet with two columns, and the key point sheet with three, are space-consuming but can be easier to use and to understand than the third, which is, however, better for detailed analysis but requires some indication of what parts of the body are used (see Figs. 3.2, 3.3 and 3.4).

Shorthand

Most practitioners use some form of shorthand, even in the finished copy which is kept for the purposes of record. Its exact nature will depend upon the conventions of the company and will often be derived from one of the forms of 'predetermined motion study' about which more later.

   The following are recommended for general use, since they are easy to follow and save some time at the analysis stage even if they are written out in full in the finished copy.

LH	left hand	N	needle
RH	right hand	pf	presser foot
BH	both hands	pfu	presser foot up
		pfd	presser foot down

It is often useful to be able to write in more detail when studying the actions of the fingers. In this case left thumb is 'LT,' left index finger is 'LI' and so on. A grasp between the left thumb (on top) and the left index finger is written 'LT/LI'.

Operation	Layout Tumblebox
SEW CENTRE ROW COLLAR	C/V
Operative **Time & Date**	Fence
J.L. Brown 09.30. 02.08.95	Operative

ELEMENT	KEY POINTS
Position collar at needle & sew on	Sew on at step 2 mm from edge No visible tolerance.
Sew centre row, sew off in chain.	Pull plies taut near points.
Clip collars and stack	Left hand holds collars. Right hand clips and stacks.

Fig. 3.2   An example of a simple record of methods.

Operation		Layout	
Sew Centre Row Collars			

Operative	Time & Date
J.L. Brown	*09.30. 12.07.95.*

Equipment & Work Aids

Brother VX 1200 (2 mm comp. foot)

Quality Spec.	Basic Time
Seam Allce. 2 mm	*2.00 b.m.*
± 0	

Layout:
Tumblebox
Fence *Needle* *C/V*
Operative

LEFT HAND	ATTENTION POINTS	RIGHT HAND
		Pick up one collar
Position at needle	*Press seam flat & hold lining away from ply*	*Position at needle*
Guide collar forward	*Stitch a seam 2 mm to right of edge from front edge of collar band*	*Guide collar forward*
ditto	*Stitch past leaf, stop needle up. Pull down ply from point &, holding it taut, stitch on.*	*ditto*
ditto	*Stitch to within 7 cm of step, stop, needle up, & pull ply back from point.*	*Guide collar forward & then pull ply taut.*

Fig. 3.3 An example of a three column record of methods.

The attitude of the hand can be indicated by 'pu' for palm up or 'pd' for palm down. Similarly 'mc' stands for machine, 'bt' for back tack and 'LHS' for left hand side.

Shorthand of this sort should normally be translated in the fair copy.

Readers may encounter some other symbols derived from 'MTM', a form of 'predetermined motion study':

P/U or PU for pickup.   P/A or PA for put aside
                          Disp. for dispose
P for position   M for move
G for grasp   CG for contact grasp
RG for regrasp   PG for pinch grasp
etc.

Readers are advised to use them with caution if at all.

Department	Section	Time Date
Shirts	Betty's	09.30 04.07.95

Garment		Size Range
Bluff Collar Nylon Shirt 178/3		all

Operation	Operative	Observer
Centre Row Collar	J.L. Brown	A.J.C.

METHOD SUMMARY   Collars are sewn in chain & ply pulled tight over points. Bundle pulled back, clipped & stacked in lap.

T.S. Ref.

Sh/1098/1

Machine

Brother VX 1200
2 mm compensating
foot

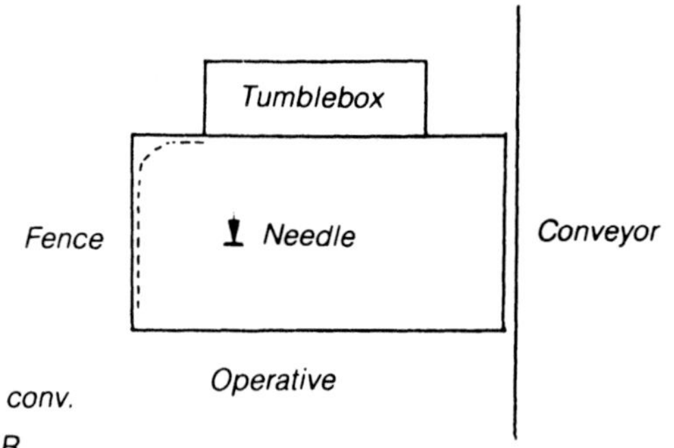

Tumblebox

Fence   ⬆ Needle   Conveyor

DETAILS OF METHOD

E1 Hand

Operative

1   RH   gets collar from box on conv.

2   BH   P. collar @ N., neck to R.,

    LH   L 3&4 spread to L. of N. L2 to R. of N. Ready to guide

    RH   R1 presses seam flat, R234 hold ply away from lining.

Fig. 3.4   An example of a detailed record of methods.

Practical aspects

Machining and handling

In most operations machining is the productive part of the job. It may, however, only take place for a fifth of the time! The rest may be spent in clerical work and 'handling', mainly 'handling'. If we can reduce the proportion of the time spent in these two activities we can generally improve the efficiency of the operative. Handling also takes place during sewing and may restrict the speed of sewing or interrupt it.

Typical sequence of an operation

(1) Undo bundle.
(2) Attend to tickets, etc.
(3) Pick up pieces of material and present to needle.

(4)   Feed in cloth as sewing takes place.
(5)   Cut thread and trimmings.
(6)   Dispose of the finished article.
(7)   Close up bundle and move to the next workstation.

Bundles

The nature of the bundle depends upon a number of factors: weight, bulk, protection from soiling, creasing and mechanical damage, etc. At the workplace we are mainly concerned with how accessible the garment parts are to the machinist.

Clerical

Can we cut down or stop writing in books, cutting out tickets, etc. and can we make the job easier by, for example, putting the bundle ticket in a holder on the outside of the bundle box?

Pick up and present

Can we present work to the machine so that it can be sewn off the carrier, the first parts to be sewn on top, labels in boxes ready for the dispenser and so on?

Feed

Does the operative have to compensate for an inefficient machine? Is a compound feed justified? What other gadgets would help?

Cut thread and trimmings

Modern lockstitch machines have integrated thread cutters but often cannot deal with trimmings. Overedge machines are less often fitted with automatic thread cutters and severing the chain, using the trimming knife, can be very wasteful in operative time and in thread. Because of poor machine adjustment or even because the machinists pull the thread to one side (as was correct on the old machines) thread is cut at the machine and then trimmed at a later stage.

Dispose

An example of the savings possible by simple adjustments in method was the sewing of a breast pocket on an overall. The first machinist sewed a part, pulled it back, cut the thread and placed it on a pile of others, ready for bundling for the next operation. The next machinist did the same and the third took the finished pockets and attached them. This was changed, so that the first machinist sewed the whole set of pockets 'in chain' and allowed them to fall into a bin on the front of the work bench. The next machinist pulled the pockets from the bin, now clipped to the side of he bench, sewed them through in chain and let them fall into a second bin. The third machinist pulled out the pockets and put the second under a knee-operated clamp with the left hand, holding the first pocket in the right hand. The threads were automatically cut as the clamp closed. The first pocket was then attached, the process being repeated until the bundle was complete. This saved a quarter of the work content of the three operations.

Close and move bundle

Putting things back in order for the next operation can often be very time-consuming. Of course, the type of bundle affects this but quite simple things like changing the sequence or using cutters' clamps can often make a great deal of difference.

Movement to the next workplace or to the rack can take up a lot of time. Major changes in production systems may be for the consideration of specialists. It is up to the line management to make their views known and, in any case, minor modifications like stacking boxes on wheeled bases, instead of moving them one at a time, might be possible without making major changes to the system.

Check list

	What?	Where?	When?	Why?	How?	Who?
Method studied						
Alternatives						
Improvements						
Consequences						

4

Basic Work Measurement

Introduction

Work Measurement

There are two main systems of primary work measurement in use. One depends upon the ability of a trained Work Study practitioner to decide what is the *rate of working* as well as the *time taken*. This is known as *Time Study*. The other relies upon the methods used, on the understanding that, for a given method, there is only one standard time. The basic data, which refer to the movements which go to make up the method, were derived from extensive and controlled time studies. This is known as *Predetermined Motion Time Study* or 'PMTS'. There are various proprietary systems in use in the industry.

Garment synthetics

This is a third method of establishing standard times. Time study or PMTS can be used to build up a library of *garment synthetics* for a given factory. These assume that the work places remain unchanged and must be updated if these are altered. Each common operation on a garment, within certain constraints such as the length of a seam, should take about the same standard time. Each style will consist of a number of such operations in a particular combination.

It is particularly useful where styles change frequently and operatives only reach standard performance after a significant proportion of the run. With this approach rates can be set from a sample garment.

Time Study sequence

(1) Check the records for operatives who usually perform at about 100

BSI on the operation.
(2) Check with the supervisor.
(3) Meet with the operatives and explain what you are going to do.
(4) Carry out an outline Method Study on each operative.
(5) Define the elements and select the operatives for the Time Study.
(6) Time and rate.
(7) Use the observed rating and times, together with the allowances, to calculate the standard time for the operation.
(8) Update the records.
(9) Install the rate.

Of course the sequence described is that for the establishment of the official standard time for a job by a WSO, but different types of study by different people will or should follow the same general pattern.

Work Measurement: its part in your job

The essential management tool

Work Measurement gives management a unit by which work can be measured and so it can be used for costing together with ways in which production efficiency can be assessed. It is also a key part of most modern incentive schemes and, equally important, the unit by which we balance factories and lines. Managers do not need to be able to set accurate rates and nor do supervisors, quality staff, trainers or engineers. But they must have a clear understanding of the meaning of the words 'standard minute' and be able to use it in their jobs, for:

- translating sms into targets for operatives;
- balancing lines;
- making capacity checks;
- checking the efficiency of one method for an element against another;
- costing the benefits of work aids and new machinery;
- explaining payment systems to the operatives;
- working closely with the Work Study Department;
- planning production lines;
- production planning;
- siting intermediate examination points;
- interpreting the production data on which the efficiency of the production staff is judged.

Time Study

Work Measurement is demonstrated by describing how a Time Study is done, partly because Time Study is the basis of the other systems and partly because it can be learned fairly easily to the standard required by non-specialists.

Standard minutes

'Standard time' is the average for one cycle of an operation that we would measure over a typical day if we had:

- a skilled operative;
- adequate incentive to call forth the operatives' best efforts;
- plenty of suitable work;
- the workplace and the machinery for which the standard time was specified;
- output at the correct level of quality;
- time allowed for the operative's personal needs and to overcome fatigue;
- expected delays due to minor machine maintenance, thread changes etc., as specified for the unit.

The output at '*incentive rate*' is expected to be one-third above that from an operative on a fixed hourly rate in most systems. In this book use is made of the 'standard minute' defined by the British Standards Institution. There are 60 standard minutes in the hour with this system.

Comparison of systems of rating

	BSI	'60/80'	'100/133'
Hourly paid rate of work	75	60	100
Incentive rate of work	100	80	133
Expected peak performance	120	96	158

It is not uncommon to hear old Work Study practitioners refer to '100 per cent' when they mean output at 100 BSI. It refers to 100 per cent of standard output.

Standard performance

In this book 'standard performance' should be taken to be that of an operative who averages a consistent 100 BSI rate over the working day, when employed at his or her own job. In a similar fashion a '100 performer' is a standard performer and a '75 performer' will consistently achieve an output at his or her own job of three-quarters of that of a standard performer.

'Operative performance' refers to the performance of an operative when 'on standard' and recorded in the management information. The use of the term 'operative efficiency' for this is misleading (see also Chapter 2).

Watches

Time Study depends upon watches and the practitioner, in the past, had to observe the operation in order to spot the breakpoint and to note the time shown by the watch. The ingenuity used in overcoming this problem is reflected in the variety of watch design.

Flyback watches

This is the simplest and the cheapest type of clockwork watch, which was also the most common until recently. The largest dial is marked in hundredths of a minute and the inner one in minutes. The hundredths of a minute divisions are known as centiminutes. Centiminutes are easier to use than seconds for the purpose of calculation. Stopwatches with this type of dial are known as 'decimal stopwatches'. The watch should be fully wound before starting to time. This is usually done with top knob or 'stem'. This knob also serves to stop the hands and return them to zero when pressed. There is a slide or second knob on the top left rim of the watch which stops and starts it. Watches should never be put away in the stopped state, since this would gradually weaken the mainspring.

As the 'breakpoint' for the operation is reached for an element, the user reads the watch and presses the top knob. This causes the hands to return to zero and to begin timing the next element. Alternatively, the watch can be started at the beginning of the element or cycle and stopped at the end. The first method permits continuous timing, whilst the other makes it much easier to read the watch.

Split hand (split action) watches

These resemble the flyback type except that, whilst one hand flies back when the top knob is pressed, the other is stopped. After the second hand has been read a side knob, on the top left edge of the watch is pressed and this causes the stopped hand to fly back to join the other which had been moving round in the usual way. The small minute hand flies back as before when the top knob is pressed and must be read before the breakpoint.

Such a watch is easier to use than a flyback, particularly for short cycles, since the observer has no need to look at the watch at the exact moment of the breakpoint. Errors in noting the exact instant of the breakpoint are more important in short cycle work, since an error of 0.01 minute in an element which lasts only 0.06 minutes is an error of 1 in 6! Where the element was ten times as long it would be, at 1 in 60, within the limits of error of the rating.

Other approaches

There were many attempts to overcome the disadvantages of the old watches. The advent of the electronic watch has rendered them obsolete.

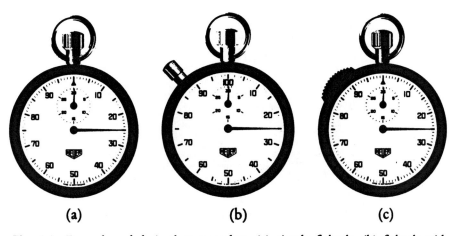

Fig. 4.1 Examples of decimal stopwatches: (a) simple flyback; (b) flyback with button time out function; (c) flyback with slide time out function. (Courtesy Heuer.)

Fig. 4.2 A split hand (or split action) stopwatch. (Courtesy Heuer.)

Electronic timers

Electronic watches are cheaper and more accurate than clockwork ones. The ultimate development is the electronic study (or 'timing') board.

These have many advantages over other timers and cost little more than a good flyback and board. More sophisticated versions can be expensive but substantially reduce the amount of clerical work involved, a fact which may not be mentioned to the manager by the WSO, who may relish the time spent in the quiet of the office 'working up' the study.

Elements

The nature of elements and breakpoints has been discussed elsewhere but the subject is covered below in detail for ease of reference.

Fig. 4.3   An electronic timing board. (Reproduced by kind permission of Eildon Electronics.)

Short cycles

Where the operation takes a short time (say 0.20 minutes) it will be adequate for a supervisor to time a complete cycle when doing capacity checks. However, for longer cycles and for greater accuracy it is better to break down the operation into elements for the purposes of study. Where a professional study exists, a comparison of the recorded elements against those of the study may show one where the time is excessive. This element is a candidate for method or skill improvement. Rating is easier over short cycles and errors of timing show up better. Uneven times for cycles may show up poor skill but they may reveal something wrong with the presentation of work, for example.

Breakpoints

Each element should have a clear start and a clear finish. This is of special importance to amateur Time Study, especially when a flyback watch is used. Audible signals are most helpful, since they enable the observer to concentrate on the watch at the vital moment.

Types of element

Repetitive
These occur in every job cycle, e.g. 'Pick up and position at needle'. Sometimes they may be repeated within the cycle, e.g. 'Close second cuff'. Most repetitive elements take about the same amount of time on each occasion that they occur.

Occasional
Although these do not occur in every work cycle they are part of the job and may occur at regular intervals. 'Bundle handling' is a good example. The time to be allowed, which usually depends upon the number of garments in the bundle, is usually taken from a large number of studies which have been converted into convenient table form or computerised.

Constant
These elements always have the same basic time. The replacement of thread for a colour change is a good example.

Variable
For these the basic time will vary. For example, in the sewing of a side seam for slips, the basic time varies significantly between full and short lengths.

Manual
This refers to those parts of the job for which the time spent machining is not significant.

Machine
This is the opposite to manual, and it is best to arrange the breakpoints so that the distinction is clearly made.

Foreign
Sometimes part of the work is essential to production but is not part of the operation being studied.

Governing
When one element is performed within the time taken for another, it is not significant to the overall time measured. The larger element is known as the governing element.

Ineffective time

It is essential, in preparing for a study, to set aside one column for activities which do not form part of the work. They may be time spent in attending to personal needs, which are covered by allowances. They may be important but not part of the job cycle, like talking with the supervisor. Their treatment will depend upon their nature and company policy. Essential communication usually falls into the 'occasional element' category. A practice which is to be avoided is to deal with them by holding down the 'flyback' button.

Timing

Start-stop

This is good method for beginners. The watch is started at the beginning of a cycle or element and stopped at the end. This is slow and only permits the timing of part of the workflow. On the other hand it makes it easy to judge the breakpoint and to read the watch at leisure.

Flyback

This is the method which was, until recently, most common in the industry. The watch is started at the beginning of the first element of the first cycle. The top knob is pushed sharply at the first breakpoint and at the same time the watch reading is noted. The hands will immediately fly back to zero and begin once again to time. The process is repeated until a sufficient number of cycles have been timed. This is called 'continuous timing' and nothing should be missed by this method. However, for short cycles which are common in clothing manufacture, it requires a good deal of skill and can be very tiring. Because of the demands of the watch some points of detail may be missed and rating may not be given sufficient attention. If the observer misses a time, it is essential that the space is filled with a dash and that the watch is again zeroed at the next breakpoint.

Cumulative

This is useful for the recording of a number of cycles by a non-practitioner. The watch runs continuously, the time shown being recorded without returning the hands to zero. It is necessary to perform a series of subtraction operations in order to establish the time for each cycle or element.

Differential timing

An important element may takke such a short period to perform that it is difficult to time. The solution is to include it first with the preceding element for, say, ten cycles and then with the succeeding element. The true time can then be calculated by subtraction.

A + b = 1.23 and C = 1.11, but A = 1.12 and b + C = 1.22

The time for element 'b' is 1.23 − 1.12 = 0.11
                             1.22 − 1.11 = 0.11

How many cycles to study?

The answer depends upon the accuracy required and the time available. The number, where the study is for the purposes of setting rates, may be agreed with the Union but this should not affect studies done by members of management for other purposes and two bundles may be enough. The time allowed for bundle handling should be obtained from records if possible, since this element will occur too infrequently in a short study for an accurate estimate to be made.

Variations in conditions may also affect the number of cycles required for a representative sample. For example, black fabric may take longer than other colours to sew to the agreed quality standard. This problem is best overcome by a number of studies carried out at intervals and preferably on different people.

It is usual to adopt a statistical approach, the accuracy of the study being shown by the variation in the individual recordings – the more the variation, the more cycles to be recorded. From 20 to 100 is generally quite adequate in our industry for establishing rates for the purposes of the incentive scheme.

Recording

Times should be recorded to two places of decimals. It is conventional to round up values of 0.0045 to 0.005 when a flyback watch is used, in order to compensate for flyback error. It is not a convention which is followed by the author, since it is entirely arbitrary. A method which is easier to use and which is still within the accuracy of the process of rate and time is always to round up halves.

Readings   0.09; 0.085; 0.12; 0.115.
Recorded as 0.09; 0.09;   0.12; 0.12.

Note that the zero is always written. Decimal points are easily missed and if for some reason a study is photocopied, extra dots can often appear in the process. If centiminutes are always used there is no need to write 'cm' or 'CM'. In any case, 'cm' could be taken for a unit of length.

Remember that the time noted are only valid for the method in use, which must always be recorded.

Timing errors

'Random' or 'breakpoint'

If the exact breakpoint is not noted accurately or if the time at which it occurs is observed imprecisely, then the time for the element will be too large or too small and the time for the next element will be decreased or increased accordingly. This is a particular problem with 'flyback' timing, since the practitioner will have to observe both the breakpoint and the time on the watch face at the same instant, but it can be reduced if an audible breakpoint is chosen.

Flyback error

This is covered above and consists of a tiny but constant loss of time whilst the flyback hand returns to zero.

Hold down

If the flyback knob is not released at once, after returning the hands to zero, the hands will be delayed in their movement and this, too, results in a loss of recorded time.

Lag

Some practitioners develop the habit of noting the correct time for the breakpoint and of then returning the hands to zero. If it is small and fairly consistent little harm is done for the time, for all but the first and last observations, is correct. The first will be fractionally too long and the last too short.

Gross errors

Sometimes the observer will omit to record the minute reading and this will be obvious if the time is compared with that for other observations for the same element. However, other gross errors may occur which are less easily detected. For this reason a comparison of the total time for the study should always be compared with the total observed times. One column may be left blank and in this the time recorded for any 'ineffective time' or 'IT'. An example would be when work is interrupted by a visit from the supervisor. After such an interuption it is usually best to include one complete cycle in the IT in order to give the operative time to get back into rhythm. A note should be made of all the garments processed in the study period as an additional check.

Fumbles

Occasionally an element time may be extended by a fumble. This should be ringed and ignored. Caution is advised in doing this, since frequent fumbles may have a significance. For example, work may arrive with an occasional pair of plies welded together in the cutting process.

Rating

In American usage the word 'grading' is often used with the same meaning as 'rating' in English texts. 'Grading' is a term used in Britain for the process by which master patterns are modified to various sizes.

Basis of rating

People work at different speeds and with varying amounts of skill. When a job is studied, the effectiveness of the operative must be assessed in order that the standard performance may be established.

$$\frac{\text{Observed time} \times \text{Observed rating}}{\text{Standard rating}} = \text{Basic time}$$

In American usage the words 'basic time' are translated as 'normalized time'.

As mentioned elsewhere, standard rating in this book refers to 100 BSI.

$$\frac{1.20 \times 90}{100} = 1.08 \text{ minutes (sometimes written as 'bm' for 'basic minutes')}$$

where 1.20 = observed time and 90 = observed rate.

Rating for the establishment of standard times

Work Study Officers carrying out a study for the purpose of setting rates for payment purposes must be exact with their rating to ±5%. For this reason they would probably not carry out the study before work had been going for an hour or within an hour of the end of the shift. They would not normally study an operative who was outside the performance range of 80 to 120 BSI. For the studies done by non-practitioners, a standard of ±10% is unlikely.

Rating skill

Time study practitioners carry out regular checks against each other and on standard film loops. Rating is an extremely difficult skill to acquire and keep. Commercial film loops are rarely of much use, since they are usually for much longer cycles than occur in the apparel industry. The manager or supervisor who wishes to understand rating properly must practise in this way and the factory Work Study Officer will normally be glad to do a study alongside the student in order to provide a benchmark. The study of consistent 100 BSI performers is best for this. The important thing is to establish what is meant by a 'standard performer' in the factory concerned. Where cycles are short, as they often are in this industry, it is recommended that the overall rate is estimated before the study proper begins. This also helps the operative to settle down.

Rating in practice

Rating for individual elements may vary from element to element and this is often a good guide to training needs. However, a skilled performer should return consistent times for each element, varying by no more than ±0.05. As mentioned above, frequent fumbles probably indicate a poor skill level or some difficulty inherent in the work. It is vital to check for these first.

Comparison of the observed rate with the average rate

The observed rate may be compared with the operative's average performance on standard. If it differs by much the reason should be sought. Some operative slow down when timed and others speed up. Some operatives take long breaks and work harder in the intervals. If they achieve standard performance it is unwise to interfere. Some operatives cheat, especially in their booking of off-standard time and off-standard output!

Rating	Comment	Speed (miles per hour)
0	No movement.	nil
50	Very slow, little motivation.	2
75	Steady purposeful movement – no obvious shirking.	3
100	Brisk pace, well motivated.	4
125	Very fast, not attainable for a working day by most people (40 miles a day!).	5

Poor performers

Low performance on the part of the operative can usually be put down to one of three causes:

- low effort;
- low skill; or
- poor working conditions.

Low effort can be spotted easily but do not confuse smooth, skilled work with low effort. Skilled work is low on wasted effort. Low skill is often characterised by jerky movements and inconsistent element times. Poor working conditions should be rectified, if possible, before continuing the study.

Rating errors

Watch rating
The speed of working is the only variable which provides a basis for rating as part of work measurement. It is wrong to choose ratings which compensate for variations in element time. Observed rate must be recorded before observed time. It is helpful to establish an idea of the overall rate before beginning a study.

Skill rating
A wide variation in times for the same element may indicate a low level of skill. One cause of these variations is likely to be changes in method, which are typical of trainees. If no skilled operative is available temporary rates can be set by a skilled practitioner with a fair degree of accuracy. One of the techniques which may be used is to ignore all but the best times, a practice which has a sounder basis in theory than would appear.

Allowances

Basis

When a standard time is calculated not only the basic times but the allowances are used. Although they are built into the time for a single garment it is assumed that they represent activities which may take up to half an hour or so but which occur at intervals during the working day. This means that the number of garments produced during a study will be greater than that indicated by the standard minute value would suggest, since there will probably be few breaks during the recorded time.

Allowances should be based on the guidelines published by bodies such as the International Labour Office and statistical analysis of studies carried out in the plant. The analysis should be updated regularly. Alternatively they may be supplied by a reputable firm of consultants who specialise in this industry.

Personal and fatigue

No one works hard all day. There are occasions when most people like to get up from their machines and take a break. You canot expect operatives to go for long periods without going to the lavatory. The amount of time devoted to non-productive activity will vary from person to person, as will the rate at which they work. The slogger, who stays at a job for most of the time at a 90 BSI rate, may produce no more than the person who goes at a 140 rate for short spells, with breaks between. The personal and fatigue allowance caters for both and ensures that proper incentives are combined with some freedom of action. This allowance is applied to all production operations but may be greater for heavy work than for light.

Machine delay

All work which involves machinery will be subject to delays which will vary with the complexity of the machinery and the level of maintenance. Where major delays occur, because of the need to call in the mechanic, the operative should be taken off standard unless a similar machine is available. However, in most modern factories there are some maintenance tasks which the operatives perform, such as needle changing. These will normally follow a set pattern and provision can be made for the time involved by means of allowances. These are given only for elements which consist primarily of time when the machine is running.

Thread change

The time involved in changing the thread will vary from factory to factory and from style to style. Where it is regular or where bobbin and cop changes are not due to colour change, then it is usually built into the machine delay allowance.

Contingency

In some factories minor interruptions occur fairly regularly. It is easier to cover them by a contingency allowance than to have operatives clocking on and off standard for short periods.

Style

Where style variations occur at regular intervals, the standard time is calculated on the rate of work mid-run. Where styles may be on a line for variable periods, e.g. 1 day to 5 weeks, it is normal to provide a style allowance. This may be in two or more parts where the length of run varies considerably, e.g. 100 per cent for the first day, 50 per cent for the rest of the first week, 20 per cent the rest of the first month and 10 per cent for the second. This is because even experienced operatives require some time to work up to full speed on a new style.

Although it is normal to build in the style allowance to the standard time, it is unwise. It is recommended instead that a true standard time should be established and then for a declining style allowance to be added to it. Otherwise problems can arise if the length of run changes to a marked degree.

Standard time calculation

Basic time ('normalised time' in America)

$$\text{Basic time} = \frac{\text{Observed rate}}{100} \times \text{Observed time}$$

First the basic time for each observation of each element is calculated. Then the average basic time for each element is obtained from this. Readers may be tempted to multiply the average observed rate by the average observed time for an element. This will give the wrong answer. A memory calculator may be used for the work, committing each individual basic time to memory as it is calculated. This will not only give a total for the element automatically but saves a column on the study sheet for each element set out. There is never much room on such sheets and cramping the space means smaller figures and a greater chance of error.

Machine delay allowances

These are applied to the total basic time for those elements which are primarily concerned with the operation of machinery.

Typical machine delay allowances (including bobbin and cop replacement)	
Single needle lockstitich	9%
Twin needle lockstitch	14%
Three thread overlock	7%
Four thread overlock	9%
Five thread overlock	11%

Personal and fatigue allowances

These, together with any similar allowances, are added to the total of the machine basic times with machine delay allowances added plus the total of the basic times for the other elements. A typical P & F allowance would be 14 per cent.

Example

	Basic time/ Element	Occurrence/ cycle
Pick up and position parts	0.26	1
Sew first seam	0.42	1
Reposition and sew second seam	0.10	1
Cut thread and dispose	0.00	1
Bundle handling	0.76	1/100

Cut thread and dispose is done automatically whilst the operative gets the next lot of parts.

Machine delay allowance $(0.42 + 0.10) \times 1.09$ $= 0.567$

Personal and fatigue allowance $(0.26 + \dfrac{0.76}{100} + 0.567) \times 1.14$ $=$

$$(0.26 + 0.0076 + 0.567) \times 1.14 =$$

$$0.8346 \times 1.14 \qquad\qquad = 0.9514$$

Therefore, the standard time for the operation is 0.95 sm.

Standard times stay the same

Performance (Rating)	50	75	100	120
Time taken	12 min.	8 min.	6 min.	5 min.
Basic time	$12 \times \dfrac{50}{100} = 6\,\text{min.}$	$8 \times \dfrac{75}{100} = 6\,\text{min.}$	$6 \times \dfrac{100}{100} = 6\,\text{min.}$	$5 \times \dfrac{120}{100} = 6\,\text{min.}$

The same allowance would be added to each and so each would have the same standard time, although the 50 performer might be difficult to rate with accuracy.

Four different people, working at four different speeds but for each there is the same standard time. The objective of work measurement is to establish a standard time for the job and not just for the operative.

Predetermined motion time systems (PMTS)

The origins of PMTS

The underlying principle of PMTS is that standard times can be derived for tasks by a careful method study. As eary as 1927 an American A.B. Segur wrote 'Within practical time limits, the time required for all experts to perform fundamental motions is a constant'. From this principle many systems have been evolved, each with its own jargon and shorthand. They are not covered here and are all derived from the original Method Time Measurement ('MTM') system, which was applicable to all industries. For each movement, within a range of distance, a time value is assigned.

The MTM system defines   eight hand movements
nine foot and trunk movements
two eye movements.

The detailed method studies, which are essential to PMTS, also provide an opportunity for method improvement. The main advantage is that alternative methods can be evaluated clearly with this technique and also that synthetic motion patterns can be constructed in advance of production runs and time values established. Like any other PMT system it is independent of rating, with its attendant inaccuracies, but subject to error, where style variation is important. Difficulties also arise in practice due to the inability of the analyst to identify movements correctly and, particularly, grasps. There are also problems associated with the procedure from 'limiting out', which arises when the hands perform different movements simultaneously.

The procedures associated with the original Method Time Measurement (MTM-1) were very tedious and, unless the operation was highly repetitive, uneconomic. For this and other reasons several sets of 'second level data' were set up. In general, these were less accurate and were based on the identification of groups of movements. From these a series of industry related systems were established, the most important in the garment industry being General Sewing Data (GSD).

Why PMTS has been so successful

In most clothing factories most of the time of the Work Study Officer was spent in 'setting rates'. Now, in most modern factories, rates are normally set by means of PMTS, with the observations recorded directly onto hand held computers so that several rates can be set in the time that it used to take to set one. The traditional Work Study Officer received a three week training on a special course and required about three months of guided experience before becoming competent. Now a former machinist can complete the training in one week and, with another week of guided experience, be able to set accurate rates, using a form of PMTS. The pay for the PMTS person will probably be half that of the traditional Work Study Officer.

Why learn about Time Study?

The PMTS operative is cheaper and faster than the Time Study Officer; nevertheless it is still necessary for managers to learn how to set rates in the original way. Firstly because all PMTS are based on time studies: the assumptions made when the system was devised do not apply in many factories. Secondly because time study is part of a wider learning, which is essential for anyone to understand the fundamentals of this aspect of industrial management. Far too often we see decisions made on false and/or inadequate premises. The recording of method blocks, by an experienced operative, does not substitute for a critical examination of the method itself. The action soon becomes semi-automatic and the brain plays little conscious part. Moreover the pattern of observations in a time study was often the key to the discovery of critical information. By all means set rates by PMTS, using garment synthetics where possible, but retain someone in the organisation, with an appropriate level of intelligence and training, to look critically at the methods and to investigate apparent anomalies in operative payment.

5

Balancing

Introduction

Key area

The managerial excess most influenced by the skill of the managers and supervisors is probably that due to poor line balance. It can be reduced considerably by anticipation and planning. Effective planning depends upon:

- a knowledge of the garment(s) manufactured;
- the way in which production can be sectionalised;
- the capacity of the workplaces, in terms both of machinery and of the skill of the operatives who work there.

The steps to a properly balanced line are:

- calculation of the labour requirements;
- operation breakdown;
- theoretical operation balance;
- initial balance;
- balance control.

Calculation of labour requirements

With good work measurement records, the work content of a new garment can be calculated. The number of people required will depend upon the probable efficiency of the line selected and the percentage of the time that they are at work and doing their own specialist jobs.

Sectionalisation

This is the extent to which the manufacture of the garment is split amongst different operations, in the interest of greater specialisation and thus efficiency.

'Operation Breakdown'

This usually takes the form of the element descriptions from the Method Study, together with the appropriate standard times and a note of the type of machinery required. Special work aids and attachments should also be mentioned on it.

'Theoretical Operation Balance'

The elements are grouped together, to match the number of people selected, in the calculation of labour requirements. No allowance is made for the varying ability of the people who will man the workstations.

'Skills Inventory'

This consists of a list of the people in the section or factory, which shows their *'expected performance'* at various types of work. It provides both a talent list for section/team manning and also a means of planning the growth of the skills of the workforce.

'Initial Balance'

The expected performance of the people available must be taken from the skills inventory, in order to man the line in a way that smoothes out the potential variations in output between the stations shown in the theoretical balance. It is usual to select *'floaters'* at this stage, who will help to cope with absenteeism and imbalance.

'Balance Control'

Balance control is perhaps the most vital skill in a supervisor, with its objective to maintain the highest output and not just to keep people busy.

For simplicity the worked examples in the text and in three of the questions in the next chapter are taken from the same case study. To preserve the anonymity of the client it will be known as 'Case Study 30'.

Basics

Sectionalisation

Within limits the greater the number of people who make a garment; the greater the possibility of individual specialisation. This reduces the training times and permits the use of special purpose machinery and work aids. It also has the effect, in most circumstances, of increasing individual effectiveness, since people speed up as they repeat the same cycle many times.

If enough people are employed in making one style, we can have several at each workstation. This makes it easier to plan for a given output and to cover for absenteeism.

For an order of any given size, more people means:

- greater efficiency *but* more work in process;
- more flexibility *but* greater space requirement;
- faster throughput *but* increased work handling.

Complicated garments will require more people if the same level of efficiency is to be maintained. In the extreme, the whole factory may make one type of garment, with variation in style being taken up by flexibility within the unit.

Simple garments make it possible to have specialist sections, who handle a particular style or type of garment.

Balancing

The problem with sectionalisation is that different operations may be done at different rates. To provide some cover against variations in output over short periods 'work in process' (or 'work in progress' or 'WIP') is provided between operations. However, if the first operation is performed consistently at a higher rate than the second one, then the work in process will build up between them. If the reverse is true, then the work in process will decline.

It is rather like trying to keep the level of water in a bath at the same height, by adjusting the flow from the tap and the outlet. If it flows in faster than it flows out, then the level will rise. Now if the outlet is faster than the inlet, we can top up from time to time with a bucket. In the same way floaters can be set to do an occasional hour's work on an operation which is producing more slowly than we need.

So we try to set the flow through each operation to be as similar as possible; checking from time to time to see how things are going; and then making adjustments to even out the flow again. This process is called *balancing*.

Scheduling

The subject of scheduling is, like balancing, part of Production Systems, Planning and Control, which is covered, in outline, in Chapter 7. The key features are:

- work content of the order;
- first start date;
- latest completion date;
- availability of specialist machinery/skills.

   The first step is to allocate enough people to an order to ensure that it is completed in time. Alternatively, sections/teams can be kept at a standard size but this approach is ignored here. The principles, however, are the same.
   It is possible to estimate the work content of a garment by comparing it with others for which records exist or by garment synthetics. The work content of one garment multiplied by the number in the order gives the work content of the order.
   The time in which it must be completed is divided into the work content of the order, to give the required output in standard hours per hour.

$$\text{Required output} = \frac{\text{Size of order} \times \text{Work content per garment (hrs)}}{\text{Time in hours}}$$

For example, in Case Study 30 1,920 nightdresses must be made in one 40-hour week.

$$\text{Therefore, required output per hour} = \frac{1,920}{40} = 48 \text{ garments per hour}$$

   For simplicity, this chapter concentrates on uncomplicated garments and, in particular, on a nightdress. Its estimated work content is 10.00 sm. There are no difficulties due to work sequence, since it is made on a transporter.

Required output = 48 × 10 = 480 sm/hour

Required team strength

For a required output of 480 sm per hour, we need enough people, at work, on standard and capable of a performance of 100 BSI.
   We take from the records the current figures for attendance, utilisation and performance. These may be modified because of other information and then become the predicted figures.

Predicted attendance	90%
Predicted utilisation	80%
Predicted average 'piecework' performance on standard	95 BSI

$$\text{Labour required} = \frac{480}{60} \times \frac{100}{90} \times \frac{100}{80} \times \frac{100}{95} = 11.7 = 12 \text{ people}$$

Floaters are required to cover for absenteeism and the problems of balancing. Calculations of this sort are not exact and it is usually good enough to decide upon the number needed purely on the basis of the absenteeism. Their performance is estimated to average 60 BSI in this example.

$$12 \times \frac{(100 - 90)}{100} \times \frac{100}{60} \times \frac{95}{100} = 2 \text{ floaters}$$

They must come from the operatives selected and so we need 10 line operatives.

Later it will be necessary to check if the people that we have chosen are likely to give us the performance that we have predicted.

Theoretical balance

Operation breakdown

First the job must be broken down into operations of equal size. The elements from the 'operation breakdown' form the basis for this. (See Table 5.1.)

Alternatives

There does not need to be one operative per operation ('operatives in series'). A long element could be covered by two or more people ('operatives in parallel'). On the other hand, one or more elements can be combined together, provided that they require the same machinery and that the sequence of manufacture permits this. Sometimes an operative can be provided with two workplaces next to each other. In this case work in process will still be needed between them.

Another form of adjustment is to move one part of an element to another operation. There are obvious difficulties and it is sometimes worthwhile to make minor changes in design in order to permit this.

An operation which is too big will become a bottleneck in production and the installation of work aids or special machinery can sometimes be justified more on these grounds than because of the labour saving. An example of this was when 'integrated sewing units' were being introduced and were in short supply. Their installation at a bottleneck operation could cut the work content by up to 15 per cent.

Table 5.1 Operation breakdown for Case Study 30.

Date: *Size:* Wms. & WX   *Style:* 2800

No.	Machine	Operation Description	Work Content Est.	Known
1	Whipper Elast.	Elasticate, att. lace & elastic to sleeves		0.70
2	O/L	Join two back seams		1.00
3	O/L Friller	Att. front yoke		0.60
4	O/L Friller	Att. back yoke		0.60
5	O/L	Join one shoulder		0.35
6	L/S (zz)	Att. lace to front yoke	1.00	
7	L/S (DF) bind	Att. binding & lace to neck & tab		0.70
8	O/L	Join second shoulder		0.35
9	O/L	Join sleeve seams	0.40	
10	O/L Friller	Att. sleeves on round		1.40
11	Whipper	Whip hem		0.90
12	L/S (zz)	Top stitch (3) neck & sleeves		1.00
13	Twin N. L/S	Yokes & top stitch each side to hold		1.00
	Sub-total			10.00

Exam. 0.20   Fold.   0.10   Press.   0.10   TOTAL STANDARD TIME 10.40

Table 5.2 sets out the various alternative arrangements.

When a theoretical operation balance is completed, then the management must check that the garment can be produced with the operations as selected.

Table 5.2 Alternative arrangements.

Operatives in parallel.	Long operations performed by two or more people.	Improved flexibility.
Operatives in series.	Long operations split.	Greater specialisation.
Method/construction changes.	The garment, the way in which it is made up or the sequence of operations is changed. Tasks transferred from one workstation to another.	May be a fall in efficiency.
Workplace improvement.	Work study and capital investment concentrated at bottlenecks.	Reduced manufacturing times.

Table 5.3 Theoretical operation balance (CS30).

Date:		*Size*: Wms. & WX	*Style*: 280

Work station	Operation number	Operation description	sm content
1	1	Elasticate, att. lace & elastic to	0.70
2	2	sleeves.	1.0
3	3 & 4	Join two back seams.	1.2
4	6	Att. front yoke. Att. back yoke.	1.0
5	13	Att. lace to front yoke.	1.0
6	5, 8 & 9	Yoke & top stitch sides to hold.	1.1
7	7	Join shoulders. Join sleeve seam.	0.7
8	10	Att. binding & lace to neck & tab.	1.4
9	11	Att. sleeves on round.	0.9
10	12	Whip hem.	1.0
		Top stitch (3) neck & two sleeves	10.0
		Total	

Example of theoretical balance

In Case Study 30 there are 10 line operatives and a section work content of 10.00 sm. All will be 'in series'. The work is done on a 'transporter' and so the sequence of operation is not important (see Table 5.3).

$$\text{Each operation will have a work content of } \frac{10.00}{10} = 1.00\,\text{sm}$$

Skills inventory

Recording the section's assets

A number of operatives are available, from which the team may be selected. The company has built up a record of everyone's performance on different jobs and we call this a 'skills inventory'. The one provided as an example is restricted merely for convenience.

The supervisor's role

Skills inventories can be made up from pay records but they should be compared with the results of 'capacity checks'. It is not uncommon to find that low performers can be brought on by giving them an operation to perform which is just beyond their expected capacity. All supervisors should take responsibility for the skills inventory for their own section.

Most will know roughly how many garments each of their operatives can produce on certain operations. Few will be able to translate this into a BSI performance.

Developing the assets

Perhaps the most important aspect of the training of supervisors in balancing is that it develops their pride in the skills recorded for their operatives. They can use the inventory to target improvements in output for low performers and an increase in versatility for others. Only the supervisor can arrange things so that potential floaters have a chance to build up their skills.

Accuracy

A skills inventory will seldom be able to predict performance to a greater accuracy than ± 10 per cent.

Example of a skills inventory

Table 5.4 shows a skills inventory for thirteen operatives in Case Study 30. It shows that Ann and Gail cannot do very many operations and none well. As far as possible they should be kept on one type of work, in order to train them up until they can achieve a consistent 100 performance or 100 BSI. A method check may be necessary.

Kate and Lyn, on the other hand, are likely to be floaters.

Initial balance

Smoothing the flow

At this stage we can try to match the work content of the operations to the skill of the operatives, in order to reduce the variation in output shown on the 'theoretical balance'. In Case Study 30 the work content per operation varies from 0.70 sm to double that figure at 1.4 sm (see Table 5.5).

Required output is 1.00 sm/min.

$$\text{Output at 100 BSI from Operation 1} = \frac{1.00\,\text{sm}}{0.70\,\text{sm}}$$

$$= 1.43 \text{ garments/min.}$$

$$8 = \frac{1.00\,\text{sm}}{1.40\,\text{sm}}$$

$$= 0.71 \text{ garments/min.}$$

Table 5.4 Skills Inventory for Phil's Section A to M (CS 30).

Date . . . . OPERATORS	SN Lockstitch	Overlock	Overlock Friller	SN Lockstitch DF + Binder	2N Lockstitch	SN Lockstitch ZZ	Whipper	Whipper Elasticate
Ann		50	50				75	75
Bel		100	100					
Cher		120	120					
Dot	75			75	25	100	50	25
Eve	75			50	100			
Fran		100	100					
Gail	75			75	50	50		
Hon		120	120					
Iris		50	50				100	75
Jill	75			50	50	100		
Kate	50	75	75	50	50	50	25	25
Lyn	75	50	50	75	50	75	50	50
Mary		100	100					

Enter BSI PERFORMANCE on Top Line.
Enter date & style then Garments/hr on Bottom Line for Initial Balance.

Table 5.5 Initial manning for style 2800 (CS 30).

Work station	sm cont.	Machine	Performance needed (BSI)	Operative	Expected performance
1	0.70	Wh/Elast.	$0.70 \times 1 \times 100 = 70$	A	75
2	1.00	O/L	$1.00 \times 1 \times 100 = 100$	B	100
3	1.20	O/L (fr)	$1.20 \times 1 \times 100 = 120$	C	120
4	1.00	L/S (zz)	$1.00 \times 1 \times 100 = 100$	D	100
5	1.00	TN L/S	$1.00 \times 1 \times 100 = 100$	E	100
6	1.10	O/L	$1.10 \times 1 \times 100 = 110$	F	100
7	0.70	L/S (DF)	$0.70 \times 1 \times 100 = 70$	G	75
8	1.40	O/L (fr)	$1.40 \times 1 \times 100 = 140$	H	120
9	0.90	Wh	$0.90 \times 1 \times 100 = 90$	I	100
10	1.00	L/S (zz)	$1.00 \times 1 \times 100 = 100$	J	100

Poor performers go to jobs with a low work content.
High performers go to jobs with a high work content.

Other considerations

- The floaters are excluded. We take note of the need to provide experience for certain people.
- We try to put people into jobs at which they will have the best chance to perform well.

Allowing for utilisation

The effect of poor utilisation is to reduce the output from the line. When we select operatives we must allow for the output lost when utilisation is less than 100 per cent.

$$\text{Selected performance} = \frac{\text{required performance}}{\text{utilisation}}$$

Required output = 48 garments/hour

$$\left(\text{or } \frac{48}{60} = 0.8 \text{ garments/minute}\right)$$

Expected output: $0.8 \times \dfrac{100}{80} = 1$ garment/minute

Allocating operatives

At each operation the work content in sm multiplied by the expected output in garments per minute will give the performance required for a perfectly smooth output. For example, at operation 1 the performance needed in CS 30 is

$0.70 \times 1 \times 100 = 70$ BSI (see Table 5.5)

Performance needed/sm = Garments/Minute $\times$ 100

Checking the initial balance

Over- and under-production is calculated with reference to the expected output. For example, in CS 30 the expected output is 60 garments/hour and the output at operation 10 is 51. This represents a shortfall of 9 and this operation is a bottleneck which must be watched carefully.

Add up the output from each operation and divide by the number of operations. Compare this with the 'expected output' for the section.

Add up the individual imbalances, allowing for sign. The answer should be the same, when divided by the number of operations. In CS 30,

'Expected garments per hour' (for operative chosen)	60.1
Expected output per hour was set at	60.0
Average imbalance per hour is therefore	+0.1

Actual output

Expected output/hour set at	60 gmts
Actual output/hour	60.1 gmts

Table 5.6 Initial balance (CS 30).

Date:			Size: Wms. & WX				Style: 2800
Work Station	sm cont.	Operative	Machine	Expected Perf.	Expected Gmts/hr	± Gmts/hr	
1	0.70	A	Wh/Elast	75	64	+4	
2	1.00	B	O/L	100	60		
3	1.20	C	O/L (fr)	120	60		
4	1.00	D	L/S (zz)	100	60		
5	1.00	E	TN L/S	100	60		
6	1.10	F	O/L	100	55	-5	
7	0.70	G	L/S (DF)	75	64	+4	
8	1.40	H	O/L (fr)	120	51	-9	
9	0.90	I	Wh	100	67	+7	
10	1.00	J	L/S (zz)	100	60		
Floater		K		60			
Floater		L		60			
Total/Av	10.00				60.1	+1	

The target 'Expected Output' is 60 garments/hour.

Plus output from floaters at 60 BSI is

$$\frac{60}{100} \times 2 \times 60 = \qquad\qquad\qquad 72 \text{ sm/hr}$$

In terms of garments at 10.00 sm each this is $\dfrac{72}{10} = \qquad\qquad 7.2 \text{ gmts}$

Total 'expected output' per hour is $\qquad\qquad\qquad 67.3 \text{ gmts}$

However, allowance must be made for absenteeism and utilisation.

Actual output is likely to be $67.3 \times \dfrac{90}{100} \times \dfrac{80}{100} = \qquad 48.46 \text{ gmts}$

This is well within the expected accuracy of the information used.

Exercise

Readers will find that their understanding of this chapter will improve if they now rework the calculations for CS 30 but with a required output of 60 garments per hour. In this case the labour can be drawn from the whole of Phil's section, not merely that shown on the previous skills inventory but also that included below (see Table 5.7). The attendance, utilisation and average performance figures are as before but, if the average performance for the operatives selected is much different from the figure assumed for the initial calculation, the number of operatives will need to be adjusted accordingly. This, in turn, will mean a new theoretical balance.

What comments would you make on the skills inventory for the additional operatives?

For what operations would an underbed thread trimmer lockstitch machine be appropriate and, if this reduces the work content by 5 per cent what effect does this have on the balance?

Further exercises, together with solutions, are to be found in the next chapter.

Balance control

Keeping the section balanced

Even if it were possible to achieve a perfect 'initial balance', changes in performance and causes of off-standard time would soon throw it out of balance. Of course, short-term changes are taken up by 'work in process' but the amount of this is limited by the cost of financing the stock and by the floor space that it takes up.

Indication of trouble, by obvious build-ups of work before a bottleneck

Table 5.7 Skills Inventory for Phil's Section N to Z (CS 30).

Date .... STYLE OPERATORS	OPERATIONS	SN Lockstitch	Overlock	Overlock Friller	Blindstitch	2N Lockstitch	SN Lockstitch ZZ	Whipper	Whipper Elasticate
Nan		110	25	25		80	80		
Olive		80			60	100	50		
Pauline		80	50	50		75		50	50
Queenie		50	80	80					
Ran		120	50	50	50	100	90	50	50
Sue		90	50	50	75	90	75	50	50
Terry			100	100				75	75
Ursula		75			100				
Vera		100				50	75	25	25
Wendy		25	100	100		25	25	50	50
Xena		75	75	75		75	75		
Yvonne		50				50	50	50	50
Zelda		80				50			

Enter BSI performance on top line.
Enter date & style then garments/hr on bottom line for initial balance.

operation or operatives sitting idle, is a warning that something has gone wrong. Modern supervision requires a more subtle approach, which makes it possible to plan ways of avoiding lost production.

Production checks

For this reason it is usual to institute regular checks of output and 'work in process'. Hourly checks may be necessary for key operations or when a new style is started. However, they are time-consuming and they must be kept to a minimum. Two- or four-hourly intervals are normally quite adequate. In the chapter on 'Production and People', the need for regular contact between the supervisor and all of the workforce is discussed. Production checks provide a framework for this. When management insist on too high a frequency of checks, supervisors will cheat or neglect their other work.

Balancing calculations

At the start of each day absentees must be noted and the initial balance amended accordingly. When hold-ups occur, due to off-standard time, it will be necessary to calculate the effect that this will have had and to see what has happened to work in process. Even the normal fluctuations in output which occur during the day may require the supervisor to adjust the manning.

Supervisors will resist the new approach. It is much easier to deal with crises when they occur than to anticipate and avoid them. Moreover, most supervisors will find that the arithmetic which is involved is new and difficult for them. The provision of pocket calculators or cheap home computers will take away most of this difficulty and quickly repay the investment involved.

A difficulty arises when we attempt simulation, by means of paper exercises. Readers become confused as to the position of the Work In Process (WIP). It is generally better to show it on the form actually between the work stations, as it would be in practice.

E.g., In Fig. 5.1,

At operation 1: the input and output are equal and so there is no change in the WIP.

At operation 2: the input is 200/2 hrs. and the output 180/2 hrs. Input less output = +20 and so the WIP grows at 20 garments/2 hrs. to 70 garments.

At operation 3: the input is 180/2 hrs. and the output is 210/2 hrs. Input less output = − 30 and so the WIP decreases at 30 garments/2 hrs. to 20 garments.

What will be the finish WIP at operation 4, if the start WIP was 50 garments?

Balance calculation sheet.

Period 8 am to 10 am

Operation Number	Manning	Output 1 hr	Output 2 hr	Cumulative output	Input 2 hrs	Change in WIP	Start WIP	Finish WIP
1	J	100	200	200	200			
						0	50	50
2	B	90	180	180	200			
						+20	50	70
3	C	105	210	210	180			
						−30	50	20
4	D	100	200	200	210			

Fig. 5.1 Balance calculation sheet.

Movement of operatives

Output is lost every time an operative is moved to a new job. Anticipation of problems is the best way to keep this lost output to a minimum and line operatives should never be moved for less than an hour except in an emergency. Even floaters should be given a sufficiently long run to work up their speed and spells of less than an hour should be rare. On occasions it is more efficient to arrange the manning so that an operative has no work to do, if this means that people are employed at the work which they do best.

Case Study 30

With the manning planned (see Table 5.5) and all operatives at work, Kate must make up the shortfall at Operation 8 by working

$$9 \times 1.4 \times \frac{100}{75} \times 8 = 134 \text{ minutes per day}$$

Lyn must make up the shortfall on Operation 6 by working

$$5 \times 1.1 \times \frac{100}{50} \times 8 = 88 \text{ minutes per day}$$

Since more people are at work than planned, they should spend the rest of the day on normal balancing and build up the work in process rather

Supervisors' Balance Sheet.

Date ....

OPERATION								
Operators	8.45	10.00	11.00	12.00	1.30	2.30	3.30	4.30
Total								
Cumulative Total								
Target								
Satisfactory?								

Fig. 5.2 Supervisor's balance sheet.

than get out more garments from the section. The emphasis must always be on keeping to the planned output from the last station.

Hon is a key operative. If she were off, Kate and Lyn together would produce only 32 + 21 garments per hour, against a target of 60. There would be a shortfall of 7 garments per hour and no floaters. As a precaution it might be a good idea to reduce the work in process between operations 9 and 10 and increase it between Operations 8 and 9. The planned shortfall amounts to only 72 and this might be the minimum WIP here, to allow for the floaters to work elsewhere in an emergency. The section 'work in process' figure is available for the disposal of the supervisor and may normally be allocated, within the section, as seems best. If Hon were a poor attender it would be best to get someone else for this job or to restructure the initial balance.

Rules for work in process

- Keep to the section target.
- Concentrate it after bottlenecks.
- Build it up when more people are at work than planned and all is going well.
- Let it fall when times are hard, in order to maintain output from the section at the planned level.
- When possible move it towards the end of the line, so that it can be got out quickly if necessary.

Guidelines for supervisors

Know   your hourly targets;
the potential performance of each operative on each operation;
the standard manning;
the permitted work in process in the section.

Make   regular production checks for throughput and inventory (WIP);
more frequent checks on key operations;
plans to deal with absenteeism and breakdowns in advance;
regular capacity checks on each operative;
manning changes based on the calculated effects.

6
Balancing Exercises

Introduction

The purpose of balancing exercises

Paper exercises provide a bridge between the theory and the real thing. Where a major change in approach is needed, practice away from the familiar eases the transition and reduces the carry-over of bad habits. Paper results are easier to check for mistaken technique. Repetition of key tasks soon renders the unfamiliar, and therefore unwelcome, to the status of a well known routine

The next step is supervised balancing on a real line. Problems occur in the factory which have not been anticipated by the exercises and any tendency to fall back into a slipshod approach is noted and can be overcome.

Exercise 1 extends the case study which has been covered in the theory.

In Exercise 2, the case study moves from lingerie to trouser manufacture, with a great deal of parallel manufacture and few types of operation per line.

Whereas Exercise 1 deals with the establishment of a new line, Exercise 3 covers in repetitive detail the balancing of a line through the working day.

In Exercise 4, the problems are the same as in Exercise 3 but with variable work in process between the workplaces.

Exercise 5 is an extended exercise in the preparation of an initial balance, using a large skills inventory.

Exercises

Exercise 1

The second team of Phil's Section (N to Z) will make most of a child's dress, work content 17.40 standard minutes, at a required rate of 21 per hour.

Predicted line utilisation	80%
Predicted line attendance	90%
Predicted operative performance	80%
Required output sm hour	____
Operatives required	____
Floaters required	____
Line operatives required	____
Expected output garments/minute	____

Table 6.1 Operation breakdown for style 7300 (CS 30).

No.	Machine	Operation	Work Content	
			Synth ex.	Known
1	Lockstitch	Mitre point of belt, att. buckle and loop, and top stitch.		0.6
2	Lockstitch	Turn hem of insertion and att. to front neck.		1.2
3	Lockstitch	Join side of collar and turn out. Hem sleeves.		1.4
4	Lockstitch ZZ	Att. lace to collar		0.9
5	Lockstitch ZZ	Att. lace to front neck.	0.7	
6	Lockstitch ZZ	Att. lace to sleeve.		0.4
7	Lockstitch 2N	Top stitch sleeves at cuff (pre O/L).	0.7	
8	Lockstitch	Att. belt loops to front yoke.		0.6
9	Overlock	Join shoulders.		0.5
10	Lockstitch	Att. collar plus tab and turn backs.	1.4	
11	Overlock	Neaten collar.	0.6	
12	Lockstitch	Join centre back seam of yoke and att. zip.	1.8	
13	Lockstitch	Att. front skirt to yoke.		0.7
14	Lockstitch	Join centre back seam of skirt and att. to yoke.	1.0	
15	Overlock	Neaten back and front yoke: join.		0.6
16	Overlock	Att. sleeves out flat.		1.0
17	Overlock	Join sleeves and side seams.		1.2
18	Lockstitch 2N	Top stitch collar to neck edge.	0.8	
19	Lockstitch 2N	Top stitch 2 sleeves.		0.6
20	Blindstitch	Close hem.		0.7
	Total			17.4

Key
ZZ Lockstitch–Zig Zag Machine.
2N Lockstitch–Two Needle Lockstitch.

(1)   Calculate the missing figures.
(2)   Produce a theoretical operations balance.
(3)   From the skills inventory, decide upon section initial manning.
(4)   Prepare an initial balance.
(5)   Comment upon the figures obtained.

Additional information

(1)   Skills inventory for Phil's Section – Nan to Zelda (see Table 5.7).
(2)   Operation breakdown (see Table 6.1).
(3)   The dress will be made on a 'transporter' and so operations may be grouped out of sequence. The work boxes go to and from a central storage rack between operations.

Exercise 2

Information is supplied for a trouser section, on straight line work (see Table 6.2).
The system is 'progressive', which means that work cannot be backtracked.
The work in process between workstations is 220 garments.
It must be maintained.
Target output (expected output) is 220 garments/hour.

Initial manning

'Serge on fly and buckette'		A, B and C
'Fob' (not on this style)		Nil
'Hang pockets'		D, E, F, G and H
'Close pockets'		I, J, K and L
'Tack'		M and N
'Pass'	(8 am to 12 noon)	O and P
	(1 pm to 5 pm)	Q, R and S

(1)   Calculate the imbalance of the proposed manning.
(2)   Comment on it.
(3)   Suggest internal movements to correct the balance.

Points to note

• Try to keep learners on one job all day.
• The greatest efficiency comes from putting operatives on the jobs that they know best and not from merely keeping people busy.
• The output of operatives should always be checked after the first hour, to see if it is as expected.
• The effects of absenteeism and utilisation do not affect the calculation.

Table 6.2   Skills inventory for a trouser line.

Top line = performance BSI Bottom line = garments/hour.

Fronts Section @ 17.12.		Serge on Fly & Buckette	Fob	Hang Pocket	Close Pocket	Tack	Pass
Alice	Perf.	100					
	Gmts.	80					
Betty	Perf.	100					
	Gmts.	80					
Chris	Perf.	75					75
	Gmts.	60					80
Daisy	Perf.		50	25	25	25	
	Gmts.		60	20	20	30	
Eve	Perf.			100			
	Gmts.			80			
Freda	Perf.			75			
	Gmts.			60			
Georgina	Perf.			25	25	25	
	Gmts.			20	20	30	
Harriet	Perf.			100			
	Gmts.			80			
Ina	Perf.				100		
	Gmts.				80		
Jean	Perf.				75		
	Gmts.				60		
Kate	Perf.		75	75	75	75	
	Gmts.		60	60	60	90	
Lillie	Perf.				50	50	
	Gmts.				40	60	
Maureen	Perf.					100	
	Gmts.					120	
Nan	Perf.					75	
	Gmts.					90	
Olive	Perf.						75
	Gmts.						80
Phyllipa	Perf.						75
	Gmts.						80
Queenie	Perf.						75
	Gmts.						80
Reenie	Perf.						75
	Gmts.						80
Sylvia	Perf.						75
	Gmts.						80

Exercise 3

Style: 2800   *Section*: Phil's   *Manning*: As C.S. 30.
(See Tables 5.4 and 5.6.)
Eve is absent.
Work in process at each workstation at start: 48 garments.

At two-hourly intervals, show for each workstation:

(1) manning;
(2) output;
(3) change in work in process levels;
(4) work in process.

Also, for one day:

(1) section output;
(2) time off standard for each operative.

Notes
(1) It may be assumed that no delays occur other than those due to line imbalance.
(2) The calculation for ascertaining work in process (WIP) levels is as follows:
     At workstation 1
     Work in process (WIP) remains constant with additional work coming from the cutting room as required.
     At workstation 2
     Change in WIP = output from previous workstation (1) less output from this workstation (2)
         e.g. @ 10 am, change in WIP = 128 − 120 = +8
         Finish WIP = start WIP + change in WIP
         e.g. @ 10 am, finish WIP = 48 + 8 = 56
(3) No operator to be moved for less than one hour.

Exercise 4

The production line is as in Exercise 3.
The work in process state is that which existed at 5 pm in that exercise.

Operation number	1	2	3 + 4	6	7	5 + 8 + 9	10	11	12	31
Work in process	48	80	48	48	81	47	67	8	37	48

All operatives are at work until midday when Lyn goes home. She is unwell and her output during the last 2-hour period was half that of normal. Hon has machine trouble and her output falls by 10 garments in the third 2-hour period.

Required
At two-hourly intervals show for each workstation:

(1) manning;
(2) output;
(3) change in work in process;
(4) work in process.

Also

(1) section output for day;
(2) time off standard for each operative for day;
(3) change in work in process levels.

Notes
(1) It may be assumed that no delays occur other than those due to line imbalance or as stated above.
(2) No operator to be moved for less than one hour.

Exercise 5

Table 6.3   Theoretical balance for style 8300 (CS30).

Workstation	Operation description	sm
1	Elasticate, att. lace & elastic to sleeves (WhEl)	0.90
2	Join two back seams (O/L)	1.20
3	Att. front yoke (O/L Fr)	0.70
4	Att. back yoke (O/L Fr)	0.80
5	Att. lace to front of yoke (L/Szz)	1.20
6	Yoke & top stitch sides to hold (2NL/S)	1.20
7	Join shoulders (O/L)	0.70
8	Join sleeve seam (O/L)	0.70
9	Att. binding & lace to neck & tab (L/Sd.f.bind)	0.80
10	Att. Sleeves on round (O/L Fr.)	1.90
11	Whip hem (Wh.)	1.00
12	Top stitch (3) neck & two sleeves (L/Szz)	1.20

Key

WhEl	Whipper elasticator	O/L	Overlocker
O/LFr	Overlock + Friller att.	L/Szz	Lockstitcher, zig–zag
2NL/S	Two needle Lockstitcher	L/Sd.f.bind.	Lockstitcher + differential
Wh.	Whipper		feed and binder.

From the theoretical balance provided (Table 6.3) and the full skills inventory for Phil's Section (Tables 5.4 and 5.7) prepare an initial balance for an expected output of 60 garments/hour.

In addition to the thirteen line operatives three floaters are required. The operations may be performed in any sequence and so operations which use the same machine may be combined. To overcome particular difficulties one operative may work two machines alternately. The aim is to obtain a balanced line rather than maximum output.

Answer 1

Child's dress of work content 17.40 sm @ 21/hr.

Required output $= 365.4$ sm/hr

$$\text{Operatives required} = \frac{365.4}{60} \times \frac{100}{80} \times \frac{100}{90} + \frac{100}{80} = 10.6 \qquad = 11$$

$$\text{Floaters required} = 11 \frac{(100 - 90)}{100} \times \frac{100}{60} = 1.8 \qquad = 2$$

Line operatives required $= 11 - 2$ $= 9$

$$\text{Expected output} = 21 \text{ gmts/hr} \times \frac{100}{80} = 0.438 \text{ gmts/min.}$$

For any operation the performance to select ('expected performance') is the work content in sm's $\times$ 0.438 $\times$ 100 BSI. (See Tables 6.4, 6.5 and 6.6.)

Comment on first initial balance (see Table 6.6)

(1) Expected output from non-floaters $= 26.4$ gmts/hr

$$\text{Expected output from floaters} = \frac{2 \times 60}{17.4} \times \frac{60}{100} = 4.1 \text{ gmts/hr}$$

Total expected output $= 32.5$ gmts/hr
Predicted output = expected output $\times$ utilisation $\times$ attendance:

$$30.5 \times \frac{80}{100} \times \frac{90}{100} = 22 \text{ gmts/hr (1 above call)}$$

(2) There is a major imbalance at operations (3, 13 and 14) of -5.8 gmts/hr. This can be made up easily (since it is a plain lockstitch operation) by the floater.

(3) Terry and Vera, both potentially 100 BSI performers have not been used.

(4) Ran is not on her best operation. The balance would have been improved if the two garments (2800 and 7300) had been made on one line, choosing the operatives from all of Phil's section.

Table 6.4 Theoretical operation balance for style 7300 (CS30).

Date: 26.6.75   *All sizes*   *Style: 7300*

Theoretical operation balance (9 operatives plus 2 floaters)

Workstation	Op. No. (mc)	Operation description	sm content
A	1 & 2 (L/S)	Mitre point of belt, att. buckle and loop, and top stitch.	0.6 +
		Turn hem of insertion and att. to front neck.	1.2 =
			1.8
B & C	3, 13 & 14 (L/S)	Joint side of collar and turn out.	
		Hem sleeves.	1.4 +
		Att. front skirt to yoke.	0.7 +
		Join centre back seam of skirt and att. to yoke.	1.0 =
			3.1 ·
D	4, 5 & 6 (L/SZZ)	Att. lace to collar	0.9 +
		front neck	0.7 +
		sleeves	0.4 =
			2.0
E	7, 18 & 19 (2NL/S)	Top stitch sleeves at cuff (pre O/L)	0.7 +
		collar to neck edge	0.8 +
		2 sleeves	0.6 =
			2.1
F	8 & 10 (L/S)	Att. belts to front yoke	0.6 +
		Att. collar plus tab and turn backs	1.4 =
			2.0
G	9, 11 & 15 (O/L)	Join shoulders	0.5 +
		Neaten collar	0.6 +
		Neaten back and front yoke: join	0.6 =
			1.7
H	12 (L/S)	Join centre back seam of yoke and att. zip	1.8
I	16 & 17 (O/L)	Att. sleeves out flat	1.0 +
		Join sleeves and side seams	1.2 =
			2.2
J	20 (B/S)	Blindstitch, close hem.	0.7
		(Note this workstation will be put backing up to workstation C so that the operative can do both sorts of work.)	
		Total	17.4

Table 6.5 Initial manning for style 7300 (CS30).

Operation	sm	mc	Performance needed (BSI)	Operative	Expected performance
1 & 2	1.8	SNL/S	79	Z	80
3, 13 & 14	3.1	SNL/S	136	Y	50
				41/60 U	41/60 75
20	0.7	Blindstitch	31	19/60 U	19/60 100
4, 5 & 6	2.0	SNL/SZZ	88	R	90
7, 18 & 19	2.1	2NL/S	92	O	100
8 & 10	2.0	SNL/S	88	S	90
9, 11 & 15	1.7	O/L	74	Q	80
12	1.8	SNL/S	79	P	80
16 & 17	2.2	O/L	96	W	100
F				X	60
F				N	60

Performance needed/sm = 43.8 BSI.

Answer 2

Serge on fly and buckette	A, B & C	220	0
Hang pocket	D, E, F, G & H	260	+40
Close pocket	I, J, K & L	240	+20
Tack	M & N	210	−10
Pass from 8 am to 12 noon	O & P	160	−60
1 pm to 5 pm	Q, R & S	240	+20
Target		220	

All but the most basic operative training must be given on the production lines not only at a horrendous cost in terms of true training costs but also in terms of the cost of poor balancing. If the team were brought up to a 100 BSI performance the output for these operations would more than double! Far too many people are employed on examining, unless they are looking at previous operations. In that case some should be moved nearer to the source of defects.

Short-term changes

D from 'hang pockets' to 'tack' as a learner, since there is a shortfall of 10/hr (under 10 BSI).

G from 'hang pockets' to 'pass', where there is a shortfall of

$$220 - [(60 \times 4 - 20 \times 4) \div 8] = 160/day = 20/hr \ (25 \ BSI)$$

K can float when needed to keep down production @ 'tack'.

Table 6.6 Initial balance for style 7300 (CS 30).

Date: All sizes   Style: 7300

Initial balance (First)

Operations	sm content	Operator	Machine	Expected performance	Expected output– garments/hour	+/– per hour
1 & 2	1.8	Zelda	L/S	80	$\frac{60}{1.8} \times \frac{80}{100}$ = 26.6	+0.2
3.13 & 14	3.1	Yvonne	L/S	50	$\frac{60}{3.1} \times \frac{50}{100}$ = 9.7	
		Ursula 41/60	L/S	75	$\frac{41}{3.1} \times \frac{75}{100}$ = 9.9	
					19.6	–5.8
20	0.7	Ursula 19/60	B/S	100	$\frac{19}{0.7} \times \frac{100}{100}$ = 27.0	+0.6
4, 5 & 6	2.0	Ran	L/SZZ	90	$\frac{60}{2.0} \times \frac{90}{100}$ = 27.0	+0.6
7, 18 & 19	2.1	Olive	2NL/S	100	$\frac{60}{2.1} \times \frac{100}{100}$ = 28.6	+2.2
8 & 10	2.0	Sue	L/S	90	$\frac{60}{2.0} \times \frac{90}{100}$ = 27.0	+0.6
9, 11 & 15	1.7	Queenie	O/L	80	$\frac{60}{1.7} \times \frac{80}{100}$ = 28.2	+1.8
12	1.8	Pauline	L/S	80	$\frac{60}{1.8} \times \frac{80}{100}$ = 26.6	+0.2
16 & 17	2.2	Wendy	O/L	100	$\frac{60}{2.2} \times \frac{100}{100}$ = 27.3	+0.9
Floater		Xena				
Floater		Norah				
Total					237.9	
Average					26.4	

Long-term changes

Train D and G as floaters.
Train the rest to at least 90 BSI one operation.
Train one operative more to replace D on 'fob' when it is needed.
Move spare operatives out of the section as output/operative improves.
Required output 21 garments/hour
Utilisation 80%
Initial target for 'expected output' at each workstation:

$$21 \times \frac{100}{80} = 26.25 = \text{approx. 26 garments/hr}$$

Answer 3

Day 1

8.00 am–10.00 am
Both float operators to replace Eve on operation (13).
Operations (1) (7) (11) are overproducing.
Operations (5, 8, 9) (10) are underproducing.
Work in process (WIP) at operation (11) will be inadequate for the next period.
(WIP = 16 at 10 am plus a change in WIP in the next two hours of −32 = total of −16.)

10.00 am-noon
Move Iris (11) to operation (10) for 1 hour.
Operations (1), (7), (10) are overproducing.
Operations (5, 8, 9), (11) are underproducing.
WIP at (7) will be inadequate for the next period.
(WIP = 12 at noon plus a change in WIP during the next two hours of −18 = total of −6.)

1.00 pm–3.00 pm
Move Gail (7) to (13) to replace Kate for 1 hour.
Move Kate (13) to (5, 8, 9) for 1 hour.
Operations (1) (5, 8, 9) (11) are overproducing.
Operations (7) (10) are underproducing.
WIP at operation (7) is now too high at 99.

3.00 pm–5.00 pm
Move Gail back to (7), i.e. the original manning state.
WIP at operation (2) is too high at 80 gmts.
WIP at operation (7) is too high at 81 gmts.

Whole day
(1) Section output ex operation (12) is 480 gmts/day, 60 gmts/hr
(2) Time spent off standard due to transfer (excluding floaters):

Iris: 1 hour
Gail: 1 hour

Floaters spend most of the day on one job and so output from these may be higher than calculated.

(3) Work in process

WIP at 8.00 am	480 garments
WIP at 5.00 pm	512 garments
Change in WIP figure	+32 garments

(4) Cumulative production

from operation (1)	512 garments
from operation (12)	480 garments
Overall change in WIP	+32 garments

Comment

Off-standard time
(a) Total attendance hours for the day = 11×8 = 88 hours
(b) Total off-standard time (excluding floaters) = 2 hours
(c) Percentage of off-standard time = $\dfrac{2}{88} \times 100$ = 2.27%

(N.B. This is off-standard time due to transfer only.)

Work in process
The WIP level has risen by 32 garments and this represents an increase of 320 standard minutes. Whilst this amount is not critical an attempt must be made to control any large fluctuations. Alice and Betty might be transferred to other operations tomorrow in order to transfer the WIP down the line.

Output
Production has been maintained at target output level.
It is important to remember that for this exercise we have discounted all forms of interruption other than those noted. Iris and Gail may produce at less than we expect because they will not have time to build up a good speed on the operations on which they spend only one hour. The floaters will probably produce more.

Balance calculation sheet

Period 8.00 am to 10.00 am

First day

Operation No.	Manning	Output 1 hr	Output 2 hrs	Cumulative output	Input 2 hrs	Change in WIP	Start WIP	Finish WIP
1	Ann	64	128	128	128	–	48	48
2	Bel	60	120	120	128	+8	48	56
3 & 4	Cher	60	120	120	120	–	48	48
6	Dot	60	120	120	120	–	48	48
13	Kate (F)	30+	60+					
	Lyn (F)	30=	60=					
		60	120	120	120	–	48	48
5, 8 & 9	Fran	55	110	110	120	+10	48	58
7	Gail	64	128	128	110	–18	48	30
10	Hon	51	102	102	128	+26	48	74
11	Iris	67	134	134	102	–32	48	16
12	Jill	60	120	120	134	+14	48	62

Balance calculation sheet

Period 10.00 am to 12.00 noon

First day

Operation No.	Manning	Output 1 hr	Output 2 hrs	Cumulative output	Input 2 hrs	Change in WIP	Start WIP	Finish WIP
1	Ann	64	128	256	128	–	48	48
2	Bel	60	120	240	128	+8	56	64
3 & 4	Cher	60	120	240	120	–	48	48
6	Dot	60	120	240	120	–	48	48
13	Kate (F)	30+						
	Lyn (F)	30	120	240	120	–	48	48
5, 8 & 9	Fran	55	110	220	120	+10	58	68
7	Gail	64	128	256	110	–18	30	12
10	Hon	51	102+					
	Iris 1 hr	21	21=					
			123	225	128	+5	74	79
11	Iris 1 hr	67	67	201	123	+56	16	72
12	Jill	60	120	240	67	–53	62	9

Balance calculation sheet

Period 1.00 pm to 3.00 pm

First day

Operation No.	Manning	Output 1 hr	Output 2 hrs	Cumulative output	Input 2 hrs	Change in WIP	Start WIP	Finish WIP
1	Ann	64	128	384	128	–	48	48
2	Bel	60	120	360	128	+8	64	72
3 & 4	Cher	60	120	360	120	–	48	48
6	Dot	60	120	360	120	–	48	48
13	Lyn (F)	30	60+					
1 hr	Kate (F)	30	30+					
	Gail 1 hr	30	30=					
			120	360	120	–	48	48
5, 8 & 9	Fran	55	110+					
1 hr	Kate (F)	41	41=					
			151	371	120	−31	68	37
7	Gail 1 hr	64	64	320	151	+87	12	99
10	Hon	51	102	327	64	−38	79	41
11	Iris	67	134	335	102	−32	72	40
12	Jill	60	120	360	134	+14	9	23

Balance calculation sheet

Period 3.00 pm to 5.00 pm

First day

Operation No.	Manning	Output 1 hr	Output 2 hrs	Cumulative output	Input 2 hrs	Change in WIP	Start WIP	Finish WIP
1	Ann	64	128	512	128	–	48	48
2	Bel	60	120	480	128	+8	72	80
3 & 4	Cher	60	120	480	120	–	48	48
6	Dot	60	120	480	120	–	48	48
13	Kate (F)	30+	60+					
	Lyn (F)	30	60=					
			120	480	120	–	48	48
5, 8 & 9	Fran	55	110	481	120	+10	37	47
7	Gail	64	128	448	110	−18	99	81
10	Hon	51	102	429	128	+26	41	67
11	Iris	67	134	469	102	−32	40	8
12	Jill	60	120	480	134	+14	23	37

Answer 4

Day 2

8 am–10 am
High start WIP at operations (2) (7) and (10)
Low start WIP at operation (11)
Move floaters first and try to bring high WIP from start to end of line whilst ensuring that no-one runs out of work.

Gail and Iris are producing faster than the preceding stations and so will eat into their WIP

Move Kate to operation (2) for 1 hour, then to operation (3 and 4) for 1 hour.
Move Lyn to operation (10) for 2 hours.
WIP bulge has moved down to operation (6).
WIP at operation (11) is still low.

10 am–12 noon
Move Lyn to operation (6) to move bulge down.
Move Kate to operation (10) to provide WIP for operation (11).
But Lyn's output falls to half capacity for this period so that WIP at operation (6) reduces less than expected and WIP falls only to 41.
Smaller WIP bulges at operation (5, 8 and 9) and (12).

1 pm–3 pm
Lyn has gone home.
Move Kate to operation (13).
WIP bulge at operation (5, 8 and 9) at 137 garments.
Smaller WIP bulges at operation (12).
WIP operation (11) is now inadequate at 8 garments.

3 pm–5 pm
Move Kate to operation (10) for 1 hour, then the operation (5, 8 and 9) for 1 hour.
WIP operation (11) still inadequate at 8 garments.

Whole day
(1) Section output is ex-operation (12) at 480 garments/day.
(2) Time spent off-standard (on transfer)   0
(3) Work in process at finish   544 garments
    Work in process at start   512   "
    Change in work in process   32   "

Cumulative production ex first station	512	"
" " ex last station	480	"
Change in work in process	32	"

Balance calculation sheet

Period 8.00 am to 10 am

Second day

Operation No.	Manning	Output 1 hr	Output 2 hrs	Cumulative output	Input 2 hrs	Change in WIP	Start WIP	Finish WIP
1	Ann	64	128	128	128	–	48	48
2	Bel	60	120+					
1 hr	Kate (F)	45	45=					
			165	165	128	−37	80	43
3 & 4	Cher	60	120+					
1 hr	Kate (F)	38	38=					
			158	158	165	+7	48	55
6	Dot	60	120	120	158	+38	48	86
13	Eve	60	120	120	120	–	48	48
5, 8 & 9	Fran	55	110	110	120	+10	47	57
7	Gail	64	128	128	110	−18	81	63
10	Hon	51	102+					
	Lyn (F)	21	42=					
			144	144	128	−16	67	51
11	Iris	67	134	134	144	+10	8	18
12	Jill	60	120	120	134	+14	37	51

Balance calculation sheet

Period 10.00 am to midday

Second day

Operation No.	Manning	Output 1 hr	Output 2 hrs	Cumulative output	Input 2 hrs	Change in WIP	Start WIP	Finish WIP
1	Ann	64	128	256	128	–	48	48
2	Bel	60	120	285	128	+8	43	51
3 & 4	Cher	60	120	278	120	–	55	55
6	Dot	60	120+					
	Lyn (F)	45/2	45=					
			165	285	120	−45	86	41
13	Eve	60	120	240	165	+45	48	93
5, 8 & 9	Fran	55	110	220	120	+10	57	67
7	Gail	64	128	256	110	−18	63	45
10	Hon	51	102+					
	Kate (F)	32	64=					
			166	310	128	−38	51	13
11	Iris	67	134	268	166	+32	18	50
12	Jill	60	120	240	134	+14	51	65

Balance calculation sheet

Period 1 pm to 3 pm

Second day

Operation No.	Manning	Output 1 hr	Output 2 hrs	Cumulative output	Input 2 hrs	Change in WIP	Start WIP	Finish WIP
1	Ann	64	128	384	128	–	48	48
2	Bel	60	120	405	128	+8	51	59
3 & 4	Cher	60	120	398	120	–	55	55
6	Dot	60	120	405	120	–	41	41
13	Eve	60	120+					
	Kate (F)	30	60=					
			180	420	120	–60	93	33
5, 8 & 9	Fran	55	110	330	180	+70	67	137
7	Gail	64	128	384	110	–18	45	27
10	Hon	51						
		–10 Gmts	92	402	128	+36	13	49
11	Iris	67	134	402	92	–42	50	8
12	Jill	60	120	360	134	+14	65	79

Balance calculation sheet

Period 3 pm to 5 pm

Second day

Operation No.	Manning	Output 1 hr	Output 2 hrs	Cumulative output	Input 2 hrs	Change in WIP	Start WIP	Finish WIP
1	Ann	64	128	512	128	–	48	48
2	Bel	60	120	525	128	+8	59	67
3 & 4	Cher	60	120	518	120	–	55	55
6	Dot	60	120	525	120	–	41	41
13	Eve	60	120	540	120	–	33	33
5, 8 & 9	Fran	55	110+					
1 hr	Kate (F)	41	41=					
			151	481	120	–31	137	106
7	Gail	64	128	512	151	+23	27	50
10	Hon	51	102+					
1 hr	Kate (F)	32	32=					
			134	536	128	–6	49	43
11	Iris	67	134	536	134	–	8	8
12	Jill	60	120	480	134	+14	79	93

Answer 5

First initial balance

Operation	Machine	Required Performance	Operative	Performance	Match
1	WhEl.	90	Ann	75	−15
2	O/L	120	Bel	100	−20
7	"	70	Queenie	80	+10
8	"	70	Terry	100	+30
		260		280	+20
3	O/LFr	70	Cher	120	+50
4	"	80	Hon	120	+40
10	" '	190	Wendy	100	−90
		340		340	0
5	L/Szz	120	Dot	100	−20
12	"	120	Jill	100	−20
	"	0	Lyn	75	+75
		240		275	+35
6	2NL/S	120	Eve	100	−20
9	L/Sd.f.bind	80	Gail	75	−5
11	Whipper	100	Iris	100	0

Prepare a table as above, trying to achieve a balance within one machine group. If this is not possible, try to balance similar groups. Tick each operative as she is allocated, attempting to put them on the jobs which they do best.

Then see what will happen in practice. There is an excess performance of 20 on operations 2, 7 and 8. Terry can do Whipper Elasticate at a 75 performance and so she can take up the slack on operation 1. Lyn has about half her time free on operations 5 and 12. She has a 75 performance on 2NL/S and so this can overproduce unless we provide a spare machine for Dot, so that she can help out on operation 9. Kate, Lyn and Sue are the floaters, whilst Ran goes onto a line with plenty of lockstitch operations.

7

Production Systems, Planning and Control

Production systems

'If a system is working, leave it alone, don't change anything'
John Gall

This is a subject which is seldom considered in an analytical fashion. We read articles on the latest 'system' on sale from a manufacturer or installed by a firm of consultants, and have to compare the package with others which have been equally extolled. We need a mechanism to do this. We also need to understand the characteristics of the component parts, so that we can see if they are right for our product, with our production organisation, in our part of the world.

The basic components of a production system:
- the degree of sectionalisation
- bundle type and size
- method(s) of movement and storage
- production flow and storage pattern
- control

The degree of sectionalisation

It is only by specialisation that modern manufacturing can work. However there are advantages and disadvantages to increasing specialisation, that is, the sectionalisation of a production process.

Greater
- personal productivity
- scope for specialised work places, mechanisation and computerisation
- speed of training the operatives

but

Increased
- need for supervision and formality of work structure
- bundle handling
- work in process, to balance the output from individual work places
- difficulty in identifying the source of defects
- chance of defect manufacture before discovery
- dissociation of the worker from the finished product
- throughput time
- complexity of production systems

and

Decreased
- flexibility of make
- speed of reaction to changing demand

We need to seek a degree of sectionalisation which gives us the best compromise from 'make through', through clump or team working to full sectionalisation. There are natural 'break points' (as discussed in the chapter on work study) which stop us reducing the time for an operation below a certain limit.

Bundles

A bundle is a number of garments which are processed together. The larger the bundle the smaller the bundle handing time, but the greater the work in process, its weight and size. Usually bundles contain only garments to be sewn with the same thread and trimmings. The main requirement of a bundle are:

> security – freedom from creasing and soiling – accessibility

Tied bundles
Traditional in men's outerwear but time is wasted in tying and untying, plus looking for parts; the garments become creased and soiled. The cheapness of offcuts, which are used as ties, is the only apparent advantage.

Sewing in chain
For certain operations this is a very cheap and low labour cost approach. The chain is fed to a bin in the front of the machine stand and removed from it by the next operative. The chain from several operations can be cut in one go.

Bags
Quite commonly used where bundles are large and creasing is not important, as in sock manufacture. Often the larger bags are dragged along the floor, become torn and then let in dirt.

Pocketed bags
Still used, for small parts and trimmings, in simple hanging systems. They are better than tied bundles but are less accessible than pegs and clips. They prevent contamination by lint and thread from foreign material.

Boxes and baskets
Some creasing results from storage in these types of bundle, but they are useful with belt conveyor systems and chutes. A pocket is usually placed on the outside, which holds the documentation. Frames, equipped with wheels, can be fitted to some stackable types. The assembly then becomes a trolley and so provides many of the advantages of both approaches. Stacks of boxes can become the storage in a PBU (see below).

Clamps on rails
For long garments these permit sewing without removing the garment from the clamp. Finishing trouser bottoms is a good example (Fig. 7.1).

Clamps on cords
Originally we bought clothes pegs and tied them to nylon cord, which was then attached to a diabolo, which ran on an overhead rail system. Now patent devices are available, with an eccentric grip, which releases the garment part as it is lifted. Those sold by Swiftrack are typical. The operative can pull the cord toward the machine and sew 'off the rail', as with the trousers mentioned above (Fig. 7.2).

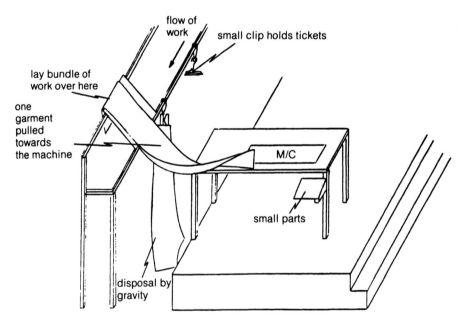

Fig. 7.1 Clamps on overhead rails.

Fig. 7.2 Manual hanging rail (clips on chains). Reproduced by kind permission Swiftrack Ltd.

Bundle trucks
Generally, these are of two types: the big, wheeled laundry bins, e.g. for large bundles of jeans, after sewing and before stone washing; or the clamp trolleys which serve the previous sewing operations, legs being held by clamps and the other parts being stored in clamps or in boxes attached to the trolley.

The containers for bundles may, like bundle trolleys, be also the means of conveyance.

Method(s) of movement and storage

Originally all work was carried from one person to another by hand. Now it may be conveyed by gravity or by some form of power as well, as a way of saving labour.

By hand — single garments, tied bundles, garments in bags and boxes

By chute or roller conveyor — as by hand but usually boxes

By trolley — wheels set under boxes, clamp trucks, wheeled bins, combination trolleys

By rail   —   hangers with clamps, boxes or
                                               combinations.

Production flow types – one way

These may be divided into one way (or 'progressive') and two way
systems (Fig. 7.3). With the one way systems it is not possible to transport
garments back to previous operations: they must be transported by hand
or by some other method. This makes it difficult, when producing the
initial balance, to combine different operations done by the same type of
machine or which require similar skills. Repairs pose a similar problem,
as does the transfer of work to a floater.

The straight line could be work stations set up on either side of a belt
conveyor. There is thus a very small amount of work in process between
stations, if any. Up to three work stations can do the same task. In a
progressive line, a limited amount of storage occurs after each work
station and this can take the form of gravity chutes or work boxes,
attached to the front of a machine stand, into which the work is chained.
The progressive bundle unit or 'PBU' has a common storage system for all
the work stations engaged in a single task. There is a progression from
inflexibility and low work in process to higher flexibility and higher work
in process.

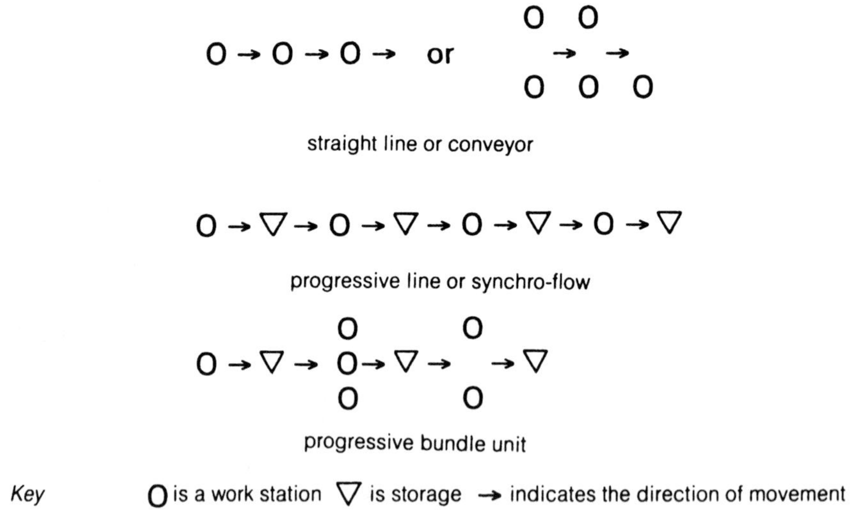

straight line or conveyor

progressive line or synchro-flow

progressive bundle unit

Key   O is a work station   ▽ is storage   → indicates the direction of movement

Fig. 7.3   The main one way types of production flow.

Production flow types – two way

There are two main types, with a sub-type of interflow, in which garments
go around a circular route until they reach their addressed destination
('selector type of interflow') (Fig. 7.4).

central storage

interflow

selector type

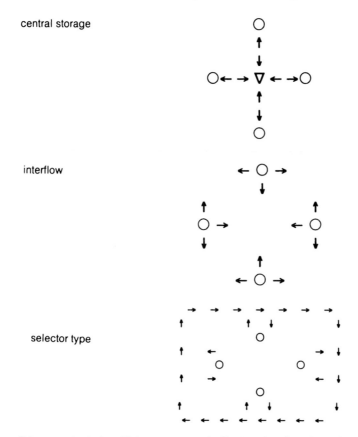

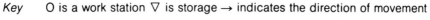

Key   O is a work station ▽ is storage → indicates the direction of movement

Fig. 7.4 The main two way types of production flow.

The central storage approach can be as simple as a table, on which sit bundles of work, surrounded by work stations. The main problem with this is that bundles are not dealt with in date order. A more sophisticated version is a central pool of bundle trolleys, with each type of machine grouped together around this store. Another and satisfactory alternative is the 'SATRA conveyor' type: the work is stored in a block of gravity roller conveyors, one for each operation, and delivered to the work stations by means of a selector conveyor belt which can be controlled to deliver a bundle to the appropriate work station. The completed work is returned to the rear of the store by the underside of the belt, feeding a gravity roller conveyor (Fig. 7.5).

The interflow approach allows movement between every work station and the bundle trolley central storage system can be considered under this heading, if the work storage occurs mainly at the work stations. A comparatively new approach is the use of robot trolleys. The selector type is usually a ring of overhead rail, with sidings at each work station and as a storage area. The work is addressed from any work station to any

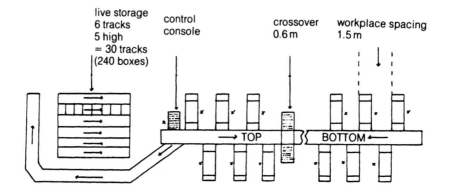

Fig. 7.5 Central storage: SATRA conveyor.

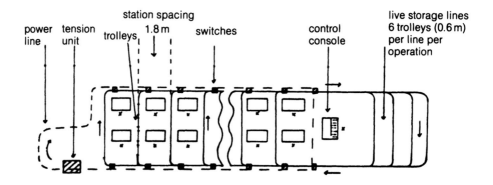

Fig. 7.6 Interflow – live storage type.

other, and this may be done by the operative or by a programmed chip or 'mag-stripe' card, with provision for a manual override when this is required (Figs. 7.6 and 7.7).

Mechanisation

The movement of work from one place to another can be time consuming, although it does provide employment for the less able or those operatives who are waiting for work. The most common method was originally the belt conveyor, but this was essentially a straight line system and restricted output to that of the slowest worker. In fact it soon became usual to leave off the power and for the operatives to slide the bundles of work forward themselves, in order to provide flexibility. Overhead rails now provide the most common method of transportation, since they are economical in

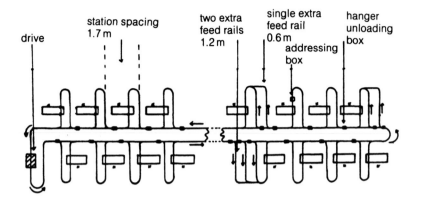

Fig. 7.7 Interflow – selector type.

space, relatively safe, and permit garments and parts to be hung (with a consequent reduction in creasing and ease of access). It is comparatively easy to link them to a computerised control system. Where a substantial amount of storage is required, it is convenient to lift bundles to near roof height and to let them flow forward on a gravity rail, as bundles are taken off at the bottom. A typical application would be the bundles of work which have been prepared for sewing after cutting. The dangers of over-sophistication are illustrated by a large company which bought an expensive and complicated computerised supply system, which occupied valuable space, when a gravity rail would have done the same job at a fraction of the cost.

Computerisation

Most modern computerised approaches are linked to a mechanised hanging rail type. The generic name 'Unit Production System' was much in vogue in the 1980s. In some there is a link with balancing, although the supervisor's intervention is necessary to a greater or lesser extent. For most the access to parts is excellent, the 'Eton Type' being distinguished by the care devoted to this. A feature of many is some means for the operative to call for the next bundle. The characteristics of such systems are set out below.

Flexibility	For ability to cope with rapid style change and balancing problems the system is unrivalled.
Little WIP	The high capital cost of the installation/metre means that storage for WIP is limited. This is claimed as an advantage and is valid to the extent that increased flexibility does reduce the need for a high WIP.
Fast throughput	A direct result of the lower WIP.

Space saving	This is partly because of the lower WIP and partly because it is a hanging rail system.
Reduced handling	A valid claim, especially for 'Eton Type' systems.
High quality	Flexible intermediate examining (FIE) is possible, with rapid return of defective work to the work station concerned. FIE is a system by which the positioning of the intermediate examining positions may be changed frequently, in order to respond to changing defect generation patterns.

Production planning and control

What supervisors and managers should know about it

Balancing is really only the last stage in the planning and control of production. Scheduling, which precedes balancing, has already been mentioned. A detailed knowledge is really only required by specialists and senior management. Nevertheless, the reader will need to have some background knowledge in order to put balancing into context, and to understand the reasons behind the decisions which may be imposed on them.

The function

The words 'production planning and control' are usually applied to the process by which the flow of raw material or part-finished product is planned, regulated and monitored. The department with this label is responsible to the rest of management for:

- allocating work in the most profitable way;
- providing information as to the progress of orders and
- adjusting the production schedules to suit changing circumstances.

The tasks

(1)	*Draft guidelines*	for confirmation by the senior management.
(2)	*Evaluate production capacity*	especially with respect to specialist and bottleneck operations.
(3)	*Make long term production plans*	using the marketing plan but with modifications to suit the prevailing state of the work in hand.
(4)	*Schedule production*	in accordance with the production plan but with modifications to suit

	the prevailing state of production. Work in process must be within agreed limits.
(5) *Originate orders for raw materials*	notifying the purchasing officer of the dates on which the items are required.
(6) *Load orders as required*	to meet realistic delivery dates, with proper documentation, whilst taking care that scarce resources are fully utilised.
(7) *Monitor progress*	in order to adjust plans and to inform other sections of management.
(8) *Provide an information exchange*	laying emphasis on ease of access for management and sales staff.

The dangers

Too often the production planning and control (PPC) function is under-valued and treated as a merely clerical activity. The main areas of weakness encountered by the writer, working as a management consultant, were in:

- records   duplication and omission;
- responsibility   poorly defined;
- computers   not used or overvalued, with inadequate software and inaccurate input.

The range of scope in textiles and clothing

The complexity and importance of the PPC function vary widely within these industries, according to the variety and specialisation of the production units.

Spinning
Little specialisation in the production unit and little affected by differences in operative skill.

Weaving
The flow process goes from warping to weaving to mending. There are different types of weaving machines, with different applications and throughput capacities.

Dyeing and finishing
A typical flow includes scouring, stentering, dyeing and the application of various finishes; printing may be included.

Knitting
There are a variety of knitting machines, with different applications and throughput capacity. The production line may extend to linking or to cut and sew. Operative skills may have an important bearing on performance. Warping may be involved, as may mending.

Clothing manufacture
The most complex process; the preparation of patterns and then lays: leading to cutting, bundling, soabaring, preparation, sewing on as many as 40 different types of machines, under pressing, off pressing, final sewing examination and packing. Operative skills have a critical bearing on productivity. Quality services and work study are also involved in the flow process. The range of complexity and the rate of style change differs widely between sectors. Low work in process and fast throughput times may be of critical importance, especially at times of rapid fashion change or for seasonal work. PPC is clearly more complex in this field and usually plays a more prominent role than in the others.

Exercise

Readers may wish to prepare, on graph paper, a representation of the time scale for the production of a garment style, showing the events and activities against a time base. For the purpose of this exercise, an event is when something starts and/or finishes and so a date can be planned for it. On the other hand, an activity extends over a period of time and may take more than a day, week or even month. For example, the delivery of the first batch of an extensive order is an event, whilst the cutting of the complete order is an activity. Events should be shown against specific days and activities as blocks of time.

   Activities that occur in parallel can be shown by blocks that are set one above another. Several such plots may be combined and used as a graphical illustration, in order to make the PPC decisions easier. This is often done on a computer display, which may be updated as actual events occur, the actual dates substituting for the scheduled ones and the schedule adjusted accordingly. For the purpose of the exercise assume that the order is a small one and that, for example, all the cloth arrives together, is cut and made up as a series of single activities. There is no need to show 'first batch of cut work delivered to sewing'. The following list of activities should be included.

Preliminary events include: finalise the design, complete the making instructions and quality specifications, order the cloth and trimmings, issue standard minute values, finalise the patterns, issue the lay plan.

Production events include: cloth and trimmings passed for quality or rejected and replaced, specialised work places equipped and machines/ operatives allocated, work cut, passed and bundled, preparation sewing completed, line sewing completed, finishing sewing completed, final machine inspection completed, off pressing done, packing completed and (with a sigh of relief) goods despatched.

It is usual to leave a buffer of one or two days between the main production activities. This should disappear as the production gets under-way, unless unexpected events occur, like an overrun of production time.

Planning, scheduling and controlling

It is convenient to consider the work under these three headings, although they overlap in practice.

Planning
The long-term view: where are we going in this year or season? The basis should be the marketing forecast. Agreement is necessary about whether the production unit can cope with the expected sales, in terms of overall volume and in terms of specialised plant and operatives. Then action is required of the relevant departments: to revise the plan, purchase the necessary machinery, train staff, obtain new premises or lease off unwanted ones, buy in additional capacity from other manufacturers, etc.

Scheduling
According to company practice, work will be allocated to production capacity according to the agreed plan, as orders are confirmed, or by a combination of the two. It is at this stage that schedules, such as the one prepared as an exercise, are drafted in detail. Although all the activities were charted in the exercise, many will be routine and will not be charted.

Controlling
Production rarely goes according to schedule, especially where the work processes are complex and dependent on the performance of individuals. Orders are cancelled and rush orders come through. Inefficiency can easily occur, unless the preliminary work is done thoroughly and the routine of change is covered by computer models (or, for the simpler organisations, by graphical techniques). Balancing is part of this process.

Key factors in scheduling and controlling

Certain facts are necessary, in order to schedule work and raw material orders properly.

Throughput time/unit	E.g., in metres of cloth or sms of work/minute
Work in process delays	Where there are a number of processes, it is usual to use work in process to buffer against fluctuations in output; each will cause an extension in throughput time.

Critical paths	Some processes occur in parallel, others one after the other. Some part of any process governs the time taken for the process as a whole. This is the critical path.
Bottleneck operations	It is essential to identify the processes for which limited capacity restricts output.
Plant utilisation	How much of the available time is predicted to be used effectively and how much is likely to be wasted on repairs, because there is not suitable work or because there is no suitably skilled person to run it?
Minimum order size	This may also be related to the expected contribution per unit of the order. We may accept an order for a few of a profitable item, but only for a large number of a product of marginal profitability.
Effects of changeover	What is the expected loss of output when one style or type of product is replaced by another and what material losses occur? For example, in knitting, when changing over from a dark to a light thread, much time is lost in cleaning down, and it may be necessary to discard material which is run through, before beginning the next run.
Waste percentage	E.g. cloth utilisation in cutting, combined with the predicted loss of garments in rejects and cloth in recuts.

General capacity calculation

The procedure is much that described under balancing on page 58 of this book. For example, a factory has 200 line machinists, who work a 40-hour week. Machinist work is the bottleneck to production and the product can be made on any machine.

$$\text{Potential output} = 200 \times 40 \times 60 = 480,000 \text{ sms of work per week}$$

However attendance is only 95%, the operatives only do the jobs for which they are trained and equipped for 80% of the time (80% utilisation) and the average performance is 90 BSI, instead of the standard, which is 100 BSI. All of these factors reduce the output.

$$\text{Predicted output} = 200 \times 40 \times 60 \times 0.95 \times 0.80 \times 0.90 = 328,320 \text{ sms of work}$$
$$\text{per week.}$$

In fact, the output of the people who are not 'on standard' (doing their own job) will provide a little more than this, but it is often sensible to take a pessimistic view when calculating capacity. There are bound to be unexpected problems.

Plant throughput time

Consider an order for 15,000 standard hours of work and ignore delays due to WIP etc.

Throughput time is $15,000 \div 5,472 = 2.74$ weeks

Production capacity for the different parts of the production organisation

Of course the example quoted above was simplistic. We need to calculate the capacity of every part of the production unit. In a cutting room the area that can be cut on one table in one day depends upon the type of laying up machine, the cutting machinery allocated, the skill of the cutters involved and the depth of the lay. The depth of the lay will be increased as the size of the order increases and the range of sizes and colours decreases. It will be restricted by the thickness of the fabric, the cutting accuracy required and the presence or otherwise of a vacuum system to pull the block tight.

From these calculations we can prepare a table, which may be linked to a computer model, and this will allow us to predict how long an order should take to complete, according to the production units available. Such a table is often called a capacity or skills inventory. When dealing with operative skills, groups of workers can be treated as one unit, with a common level of productivity, and this is called a 'skill centre'. This simplifies calculations. Most of the techniques used in this type of work depend on some form of simplification. The effect of labour saving machinery can often be considered by expressing its output in terms of the number of conventional machines that it replaces.

Calculations of variation in output with style variation

An assumption is made that sufficient spare machinery and sufficient versatile machinists are available to cover all style changes. Each style change is covered by considering the increase in work content, which results from its introduction, and the resulting reduction in output compared to that for a simple garment. Table 7.1 deals with a factory with a single product and its variations.

Analysing a multi-style factory

Consider a company that makes ladies dresses and blouses. Here the

Table 7.1

Shirts/hr	variations				
feature →	plain	placket	2 darts	1 pkt	2 pkts
Fronts	60	−10	−5	−5	−10
Backs	80	0	−10	0	0
feature →	plain	simple vent	gauntlet	2 tuck	fancy
Sleeves	80	0	−10	−5	−20
Cuffs	80	0	N/A	−5	−20
feature →	bluff	top stitched	specials		
Collars	80	−5	−20		
feature →	plain	yoked backs	fancy fronts	yoked fronts	
assembly 1	70	−15	−20	−15	
feature →	plain	2N sides			
assembly 2	70	−20			
feature →	standard	extra button			
bttn sew & bttn hole	70	−5			

cutting room has little difficulty in coping with the variations in style, since the types and weights of the fabrics do not vary much over the range. In order to promote efficiency, each line is given specific groups of styles or 'garment families' to sew, as far as the production schedule will allow. The production controller needs to know just what each line can produce, in order to be able to cope with variations in demand. In the table opposite the production capacity is expressed in standard hours of work per day. This is because the style variation does not make it sensible to deal in garments. The work content can vary considerably, in a single garment family, between one garment and another. Details are provided in Table 7.2.

Computerisation

Computers can handle the arithmetic of production planning and control

Table 7.2

Style Group → Line ↓	blouse A to D	blouse E to G	blouse F	dress A to C	dress D to F
1	70	80	0	80	60
2	80	70	0	70	40
3	0	0	120	80	80
4	60	80	80	100	90
Maximum	210	230	200	330	270

Caveat
Readers should be aware that these examples are only introduced as illustrations of a principle and that more complex models would be needed in practice.

far better than clerks. The use of computer models is now considered to be essential in any large organisation. Strong selling and the desire to be 'up-to-date' creates a climate in which managers are strongly influenced towards letting the computer take the strain. Managers must beware of this and investigate what lies behind the software before they buy it. It is always essential to run the old system in parallel with the new for a period, despite the heavy work load that this places on staff. Properly used, computers are invaluable in the making of fast decisions, based on very recent information. Terminals, rather than printout should be the means of keeping colleagues informed.

The subject is covered generously in the technical press and is dealt with only in outline below. The main drive has been to reduce inventory and throughput time. 'Quick Response' is mainly concerned with the latter and is particularly important in those industries which, like ours, have a high fashion element.

MRP (Materials Requirements Planning)

This was essentially a computerisation of existing clerical techniques. It is a system of information based on the requirements for direct materials and part-finished product, in terms of type, volume and the dates by which the manufacturing unit will require them. A master time schedule is prepared for a given time period. In one approach ('regeneration') the complete schedule is renewed ready for the beginning of a new time period. In the other ('net-change') only those aspects that have changed are recalculated and represented. Its reliance on a forecast has led to charges of rigidity and, in many companies, a parallel system was run by the operating management, as an aid to flexibility.

MRP II (Manufacturing Resource Planning)

Much confusion has arisen because of the similarity between the two titles. There are a variety of versions, each with its enthusiastic supporters, notably the salespeople for the consultancy firms involved. Like MRP it is dependent on a master plan. Fundamental to the system is the injection of goods of the required type and volume, at the specified place, at the planned time. At its simplest it is an entirely rigid system and takes no account of cancelled orders, machine breakdowns or other irregularities. To the extent that it forces production managers to abandon old and slack practices, it has an important role and was much needed in a Britain that had gained an unenviable reputation for unreliable delivery dates. It was much supported in Germany and France. Computerisation of information processing is essential to its success. As time has gone MRP II has been successfully modified towards the 'Just in Time' approach.

Just in Time (JIT)

The origins of the 'just in time' approach lie in Japan. Originally a small wooden token, a 'kanban', was passed back from each unit when a batch of goods had been processed. This called forward the next batch of parts and stores. A 'kanban' was a small Japanese coin. The process soon became computerised. This system has been modified to incorporate forward planning and so there is a convergence between JIT and MRPII. Perhaps because of its Japanese origins JIT has been associated with a number of other Japanese inspired techniques, including Total Quality Management.

JIT has been likened to a train pulled from the front and MRPII to one pushed from behind.

8

Total Quality Control

Introduction

Purpose of this chapter

Quality control in clothing could form the basis for an entire book. This chapter attempts to introduce the subject at a level suitable for junior management and supervision. In particular it tries to convey the idea that quality is something that is built into a garment from the stage of market research and design right up to pack and despatch and indeed extends beyond to a careful analysis of customer returns and consultation with the buyers. Quality control is exerted by the people who make a garment and not just by the small number of the staff who are specialists in monitoring the output and setting out specifications.

Quality

This escapes definition. The term itself implies value. The nature of that value depends upon the purpose for which a garment is bought. Pure silk satin is not hardwearing but Christmas sees a lot of Mums (and other ladies) happy with its quality. Mostly it adds up to fitness for purpose, with visual appeal coming fairly high on the list of requirements, with a long wear life being more important in some cases and vital to most. It is viewed differently by the designer and the production executive and those aspects which are important to each are set out separately in the text.

Sampling

This is the process by which we take a small number of garments and examine them to see what they can tell us about the large number from which they were taken. If a sample is representative of the whole, then it is possible to monitor quality at a aminimum cost. The theory of sampling deals with the ways that we can sample in order to have the best chance of looking at garments which represent the rest and what we do when they are not up to standard. Another form of sampling is when we look at certain key features, either because they are more likely than the rest to be defective or because they are of particular importance.

Quality Control Department

The main function of the 'Quality Control Department' is not to control quality but to provide a service which allows other people to make good clothes. Their main concern must be to do this at the minimum cost, balancing the expense of the department against the savings it makes possible in terms of reduced repairs and rejects. One aspect of this is to define the quality level of the plant and of the workplaces in it. To try for a quality above what is natural for the operatives and the machinery with which they work is to invite spoilt work and lost output. The raising of quality levels requires a major project which involves investment in machinery and training and it cannot be done quickly.

The maintenance of quality at an agreed level implies clear specifications and these are an important task for this department. As far as possible, specifications should be common to all goods made in the plant. This means that the sheets for individual styles can be kept as brief as possible. They should contain the maximum information in the form of sketches and all dimensions should be quoted with tolerances. Tolerances reflect the extent to which the less than perfect is acceptable. However small, tolerances exist for all garments.

Terms in use

Quality

The quality of a garment is the reason that it is bought by the customer and comprises a set of 'quality characteristics' which together make up its 'fitness for purpose'. The key to profitable garment manufacture is to provide the best combination at the lowest cost, *'the economic quality level'*.

The costs of quality come from:

- style;
- fabric and trimmings;
- make, including repairs and rejects;
- Quality control function.

The term 'fitness for purpose' is very apt, because it serves as a warning that good quality is aimed at the ultimate customer, the person who buys and wears the clothes. Until recently, menswear appeared to be made more to impress other tailors than to please the customer. Some retail organisations still employ 'more than my job's worth' buyers, whose concern is for conformance to specification, rather than for a better deal for the customer. A few loose threads may mean less than a lower price, when the buying decision is made.

Fitness for purpose comprises:

- quality of design;
- quality of conformance;
- quality of delivery and service.

Quality characteristics

As Juran says, these are 'the basic building blocks on which fitness for use is built'.

Quality of design requires a higher level of market research than is common in our industry. One of its main objectives must be to establish what is the ultimate customers' preference, at an acceptable price, amongst a competing set of characteristics. These can then form the basis for the design. Customers may demand various combinations of the following, in various orders of importance:

- price and apparent value for money;
- individuality of appearance;
- fashion appropriate to the group and period;
- image enhancement (solid reliability for the solicitor's suit, hygienic smartness for the waitress, etc.);
- comfort in wear, both from cut and from fabric;
- durability of appearance and function;
- physiological qualities (waterproofing, warmth, sweat absorption, etc.);
- ease of care (crease and stain resistance; shape retention; washability, etc.);
- size and shape (closer fit for the formal, smaller size intervals for the more expensive and a basic block appropriate to the target group of customers);
- consistency of product.

On the other hand, the production man can do little about many of the quality characteristics except to stick to the specifications. He is more concerned with the needs of the retailers, which are:

- consistency (dependent on clear specifications with tolerances; the means to achieve the required quality level; the will to conform of Management and Workforce);
- delivery on time;
- low cost to support the competitive price.

Sampling

A proportion of the throughput of garments is considered to be representative of the whole throughput and is examined. The rest are usually examined only if the sample is found to have an unacceptable level of defects. This may be one major defect or a lot of minor ones. It is particularly useful in detecting bad work at early stages of production, so that the cause can be put right. For low value garments, of high consistency, it can also serve as final examination.

Quality control

Quality is actually controlled by the process of manufacture, from design to pack and despatch. However, the term is conventionally used to describe the process by which management seeks to monitor the quality of output, to compare it with the accepted standards and to act upon the difference. Some modern writers use the term 'quality assurance' as a clearer indicator of the function's purpose.

'Statistical Quality Control' (SQC) is a term which implies that only a proportion of the garments are examined and that these are chosen according to rules which come from the theory of statistics. It has been oversold in the past, in terms of its accuracy, and the assumptions on which it is based may often not apply to garment manufacture.

'Total Quality Control' is a name given by the movement which arose as a reaction to the over-enthusiasm of the 'SQC' pundits. It suggests a return to the idea that good quality is part of the whole manufacturing process. 'Zero Defects' and 'Right First Time' have a similar connotation. This chapter is mostly about 'Total Quality Control'.

The Quality Control Department

The department's function

The original function of the department was to stop bad work leaving the factory and reaching the customer. Modern thinking is that it is there to reduce the amount of bad work being *made*. This gives savings in the cost of the repairs and rejects but also speeds delivery. Its aim is to help people to make garments correctly the first time. When the proportion of defects is low, say 2 per cent, even if final examination allows half to reach the customer, this is still a lower proportion of the output than where defects are high, say 20 per cent and final examination stops nine-tenths (a good performance even with 100 per cent examination). In one case 1 per cent escape but in the other 2 per cent escape.

Even today, it is usually possible to reduce the cost of the quality control function *and* to improve the proportion of bad work leaving the factory.

Extra costs	Savings
Planning	Delays in delivery
Prevention	Repairs
Inspection	Remakes
Monitoring the effects	Returns

Extra costs

Planning
- definition of required quality characteristics and quality level by market research;
- establishment of revised quality control procedures;
- evaluation of sampling levels and selection of examination points;
- calculation of appropriate manning levels.

Prevention
- specifications with tolerances;
- fabric and trimmings to specification;
- appropriate machinery in good condition;
- correct methods and good training.

Inspection
- properly selected and trained examiners;
- standard examination procedures, with suitable equipment;
- rapid feedback of information, checked against results.

Monitoring
- checking the efficiency of the examination;
- seeking out trouble spots;
- comparing defect ratios with budgets;
- comparing the costs of prevention with those of poor work.

Some of the extra costs are much higher in the beginning and represent an investment in the future. It is usually best to buy in extra help for this – partly because consultants should have expertise at an adequate level for the pioneer work, which is considerably higher than that required to maintain a good system, and partly because they represent additional management when a great deal of extra work is necessary.

Some of the extra costs are outside the Quality Control Department, in better machines and training.

The most important of the long-term costs is that of examination but this can be reduced by sampling. As the quality of output rises the proportion which is sampled can be reduced, even at final examination, so that the real cost of examination can actually be less than before.

Savings

Delays
- shipments which are held over awaiting the completion of repairs require extra capital to finance them;
- if despatch dates are delayed orders may be lost;
- with the modern emphasis on 'just in time manufacture' and small inventories, balancing problems caused by repairs can cut output drastically.

Repairs and remakes
- repairs cost money in unpicking, extra handling and supervision, as well as in restitching;
- remakes may mean extra cutting and problems of shading, which result in good parts being discarded, with a high cost in wasted material;
- the labour cost of a repair is usually estimated at least half the total labour cost of the garment, to which overheads must be added.

Returns
- these may mean lost orders;
- often it is too late to replace the returned garments and the revenue is lost for ever.

Plant quality level

One of the features which the Quality Control Department must monitor is that of the 'plant quality level'. This is the level of quality which can be attained without unusual care and at an economic production rate. The term can be used in a similar way with respect to a section, a process, a machine or an operative.

The plant quality level will depend upon the quality expected of the traditional product; the type of machinery; work aids and processes in use; the usual cloth and trimmings and, above all, on the operative skills.

It must be recognised so that it can be compared to the acceptable quality level and full consideration given to any short-fall when considering production of a new style. In the short term, any production at levels above the plant quality level will call for considerable management effort and a reduction in productivity.

In the long term a *quality improvement programme* can often raise both the plant quality levle and productivity.

The plant quality level is also related to outlet. Branded garments usually concentrate on individuality and aesthetic features or on well known qualities associated with the brand, whilst those made for chain stores will have an emphasis placed on conformity and consistency, particularly details such as 'no thread ends.' Joint production by the same unit can only be achieved in a satisfactory fashion by raising the quality level to the highest requirements of both types of outlet.

Where the consistency of the quality is poor, the expected quality level is substantially below the average quality of output. We must cater for the small proportion which are below standard. Greater consistency has an even higher priority than raising the standard of the majority of the garments made, which may be satisfactory.

Quality specifications

The responsibility for these usually rests with the quality control department and they should be an exercise in communication. The minimum of paper with the maximum of information is the ideal. This can best be done by having factory standards for most aspects, which are familiar to everyone and are changed as seldom as possible. A system by which all outdated copies are withdrawn is essential. Special specifications, which relate to specific styles, can then be distributed when required and these should seldom cover more than one sheet (see Fig. 8.1).

Factory specifications
- cloth and trimmings, button spacing;
- thread and needle types and sizes, by fabric and seam type;
- stitches per inch or per 2 centimetres;
- seam types, seam margins and tolerances;
- standard blocks and size ranges;
- cutting standards.

Style or garment specifications
- items of difference;
- special size ranges and grading;
- key features and quality points;
- special tolerances;
- fabric and trimmings, colours and shades (shade cards checked regularly for fading).

Points to watch
- easy to read;
- pictures rather than words;
- dimensions and tolerances on sketches.

Tolerances

These are the limits of acceptability. Wherever possible they are expressed in figures. For example, the specification for a seam margin may be 1 cm and the tolerance ±2 mm. In some cases the tolerance may be written as 0 mm and this usually means that no error should be discernible.

Some specifications cannot be expressed in terms of figures. Then the tolerances must be expressed by examples or (at worst) photographs should be used to demonstrate the limits of acceptability.

Control limits may be set which are more severe than the tolerances.

J & B WREN LTD.			FACTORY QUALITY SPECIFICATION		
Spec. by A.B.	Approved J.W.	Date 01.06.95	Style all		Size all
Machine Type L.S. T.N. ISU, swing N		Auto jig	Operation Patch Pkt. Round Bott.		Needles as gmt. spec.
ITEM	JOB DETAILS			Standard	Variation +/−
1	Cover drill hole symmetrically			on or cover	judgement
2	Align with notch (SIDE PKTS Fig. 1A) (BREAST PKTS Fig. 1B)			see fig	"
3	Sew around pocket, using jig, parallel to edge. (Fig. 1)			2 mm	1 mm
	Second row, if present, 6 mm inside first			6 mm	1 mm
4	Corners quarter circles				1 mm
	All pockets to be die cut +/− 1 mm & pre-pressed.				

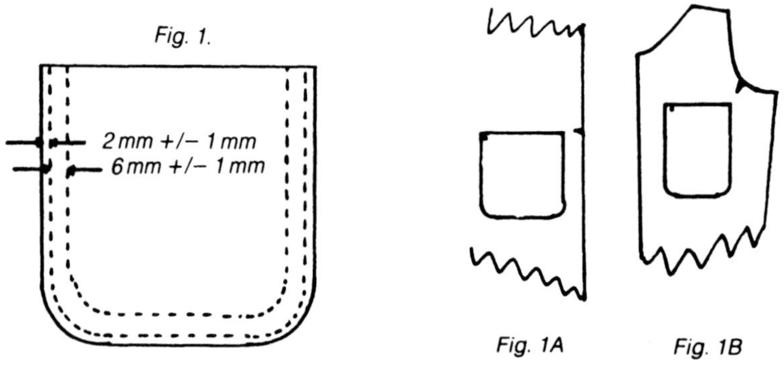

Fig. 1.

2 mm +/− 1 mm
6 mm +/− 1 mm

Fig. 1A   Fig. 1B

Fig. 8.1   Factory Quality Specification.

These define the minor defects, those which are acceptable but which may be an indication of a deterioration of the quality of performance at a given operation. Too many minor defects may cause the rejection of an entire garment.

NACERAP (FACERAP)

This is a word which stands for: 'Name'
'Appearance'
'Cause'
'Effect'
'Repair'
'Action'
'Prevention'

NACERAP provides a systematic approach to defects and is very useful in training. It is not useful to have stacks of cards made out in this way for every fault.

It helps if everyone calls a certain type of fault by the same name. Somewhere there ought to be a record of all the faults which are likely to be encountered in the factory, each identified by a name and a photograph and/or sample. Otherwise defect records may mean different things to different people. Plainly everyone must be trained to use the same words to identify defects or the defect records will be ambiguous.

Often there is more than one cause for what is apparently the same defect. Readers are advised to consult the section 'Seam pucker' in 'Making up' in Chapter 9 for an example. The most likely causes or those which may easily be identified should be considered first. The effect of each cause will differ in one way or another and it is by this that we can identify it. Sometimes it comes down to 'it is not caused by ... so it must be caused by ...'.

It is worthwhile to specify if certain defects should be repaired, since it may cost too much. There may be several methods by which the repair can be done, only one of which is best.

Specific action may be necessary if a defect is discovered. For example, it may be possible to overcome the effect of poor cutting as when shallow notches are deepened by hand. It is essential to notify the cutting room as a means of prevention but it may also be necessary to pay a premium to the operative concerned.

An example of a defect analysis chart for seam pucker is provided in Fig. 8.2.

ISO 9000 and TQM

What ISO 9000 is about

In 1979 Britain pioneered an idea which has now won worldwide acceptance. It is possible to define the quality system of an organisation, so that positive action is taken to prevent the occurrence of defects. For each organisation the system is written down in the form of a 'quality manual'. Internal assessors monitor the behaviour of the actual quality system against the quality manual. The results of their 'audits' reveal the extent to which the organisation complies with the quality manual and the extent to which the quality manual itself requires alteration to comply with the standard. External assessors audit both the quality manual and the way in which it is implemented against the standard, and, if their audit is satisfactory, the organisation is certificated. In both cases, any incidence of noncompliance is recorded and preventive action taken. When a noncompliance has been properly dealt with, the noncompliance report is 'closed out' by an appointed person. Thus purchasers who deal with a certificated firm are provided with assurance that the quality

DEFECT ANALYSIS CHART		DEPARTMENT	*OLDHAM*	Date		--------
SEAM PUCKER		SECTION	*All*		Reference	*J.A.L./1*
CAUSE	EFFECT	RECTIFICATION	ACTION		PREVENTION
1. One ply cut too short – operative 'easing in'.	*Measurement incorrect & pucker on one ply.*	*Unpick & order recut of short ply.*	*Inform cutting room.*		*Check top and bottom plies in every block.*
2. Wrong size needle.	*Consistent pucker on both plies.*	*Unpick & resew with a smaller needle if poss. If not consult QC*	*Inform QC who should change Q.Specification.*		*Smaller needle required in Q.Spec.*
3. Too many stitches to the cm.	*Consistent pucker on both plies.*	*Unpick & resew @ fewer stitches per cm.*	*Inform QC.*		*Lower stitch density in Q.Specification.*
4. Wrong direction of stitching.	*Pucker on ply sewn along warp.*	*?*	*Call QC.*		*Design.*
5. Thread tension wrong.	*Seam shortened.*	*Unpick & resew @ correct thread tensions.*	*Adjust thread tension.*		*Regular checks.*
6. Differential stretch.	*Pucker on one material.*	*?*	*Call QC.*		*Design or puller feed.*
7. Incorrect sewing thread.	*Pucker appears after washing or wearing.*	*Not identified in Making up.*	*Inform QC.*		*Correct thread in Q.Specification.*
8. Operative or mc overfeeding top ply.	*Top ply sews up too short.*	*Unpick & resew after adjusting top feed or op.'s method.*	*Adjust feed.*		*Trial sew before starting production.*
9. Presser foot drag.	*Reverse of 8.*	*Unpick and resew after adjustment.*	*Adjust presser foot pressure to minimum. On L/S use less throw or finer teeth on dog. Teflon cover or special foot. Top feed.*		*Correctly adjusted machine with correct presser foot.*
10. Fabric finish or structure.	*Pucker not covered under 1 to 9.*	*Nil*	*Call QC.*		*Change design &/or fabric.*

Fig. 8.2   Defect analysis chart for seam pucker.

system is satisfactory and likely to provide goods of an acceptable standard.

External assessors must pass an examination, after attendance at a suitable ('lead assessor') course. They are also required to complete a number of satisfactory assessments before being allowed to take charge of an assessment or to run a course for future lead assessors, and then are known as 'registered' assessors or lead assessors. Internal assessors must be properly trained and at least one internal assessor per organisation must have been trained by a registered lead assessor; that person only may train internal assessors within the organisation. A recent change has been to call 'assessors' 'auditors'.

From MILQ, though AQAP, BS 5750, ISO 9000 to TQM

Most innovations in quality management arise from the needs of military procurement. In this case MILQ – 9858 A was adopted by NATO in 1968. From this evolved AQAP 1 and its successors. A more rigorous, civil version of AQAP 4 became BS 5750 in 1979. It was quickly taken up by the International Standards Organisation and, in a modified form, became ISO 9000:1987. In Britain it was now known as BS 5750:1987. 'Vision 2000' is a document which charts the proposed future progress of ISO 9000. As part of this plan ISO 9000 was again revised in 1994 and the term BS 5750 became obsolete. The next version is due out in 1998 and thereafter five-yearly revisions are planned.

Total Quality Management (TQM)

Total Quality Management may be said to have arisen out of a British desire to emulate the Japanese standards for quality, but to adapt them to suit a different culture. It is defined by BS 7850, which suggests 'BS 5750' as a basis. Nevertheless there have been a great number of articles and seminars on TQM, which have painted a quite inaccurate picture if its meaning. The process of Total Quality Control, described in this chapter, is the main foundation. Quality Circles feature in some applications. Professor Oakland wrote a pioneering book on the subject; he applied his field of special knowledge, using the feedback loop of Statistical Process Control for the improvement of management. Many organisations which practise TQM place great reliance on the concept of good customer/supplier relations: within the organisation, between departments, and externally. It is a management philosophy and should not necessarily be administered by the quality management specialists. The key features of TQM are:

- continuous quality improvement ('Kaizen');
- total business management;
- company-wide quality management;
- cost effective quality management.

The Japanese formerly called their approach 'Total Quality Control' but even Toyota have now begun to use the term 'Total Quality Management'.

9

Quality from Design to Despatch

Introduction

'Right first time'

Real quality control comes from the whole organisation, from design to despatch and then, through customer returns and market research back to design. The writer recalls the managing director who was concerned that he might not have enough quality control staff, there being only three against nearly two hundred in manufacturing. The output, which was of menswear, had from 2 to 3 per cent defectives! The garments were made correctly and did not need an army of examiners to protect the customers from bad work.

Design and fabrics

If good quality is not *designed* into a garment it will not possess it. Designers should aim to work within the constraints imposed by the production unit. In it particular features should be incorporated, which make the maximum use of automatic machinery and work aids and seams should be specified for ease of sewing, whenever possible. Designers must be aware of the natural quality level of the factory.

The purchasing of fabrics is the job for a trained textile technologist. Proper purchasing contracts and point of manufacture testing can save costly delays at the cutting stage. However, quality control is not merely a matter of washability, abrasion testing and the like, as some authorities seem to imply.

Cutting

Good cutting makes good sewing easier. Poor cutting may make it impossible. The imposition of precise standards and the examination of cut work will play a vital role in maintaining quality levels. Regular contact between cutting and sewing staff is helpful. Pilot runs for all sizes of a new style are a good way of checking to see if the pattern cutting and grading have been done properly.

Making up

Often the attention of the quality specialists is over-concentrated on this aspect of manufacture. Nevertheless, there are more people working here than in the rest of the factory and so there is more scope for things to go wrong. Fast feedback of information to supervisors is the key to preventive quality control – making things properly the first time. Sampling at in-process examination positions can be a great help.

Other factors

Management must demonstrate their interest in good quality if the workforce are to take it seriously. One of the best ways for them to do this is to spend part of one day a month on a 'quality audit' and its follow-up.

Emphasis on the customer comes from a systematic review of customer returns or returns to manufacturer ('RTMs') and, where possible, by occasional contact between buyers and production staff.

The examination of a garment should be systematic whoever does it. It is helpful to produce charts which may be hung at examination points and which show a sensible order in which to check for defects, with the key points highlighted.

Design

Quality characteristics

The balance between the quality of a garment and its cost is the secret of good commercial design. The correct emphasis on the different quality characteristics will have been established by the buyers from the retail organisation and/or by market research. There will probably be a price range into which it must fit.

Value analysis

A comparison of the cost of different materials, which meet the minimum specification for performance in use, will frequently permit cost savings whilst maintaining the quality level. For example, a badly designed shirt may have a collar which shrinks after twenty washings, whose seams give way after forty washings and shows no sign of fabric fading or wear for some time after that! The objective of value analysis for durability is that, as far as is economically possible, failure in most parts occurs at about the same stage of wear.

In some cases more expensive fabrics can be justified because they have good performances for frayability and crushability, which cut the costs of production.

Chain stitch can be specified instead of lockstitch, where it will give an acceptable performance. Fusible tape may replace some sewing operations such as blind hemming.

Pattern engineering

This consists of modifications for ease of make or mechanisation. For example, the equalisation of the curve of the hind and forearm seams on a jacket not only makes for ease of manufacture on a long seamer but on a plain sewer as well.

Parts like tabs and pocket flaps can be standardised so that they can be die cut and jig sewn. Labels for care and sizing can be made to incorporate most or all of the information in one pattern, which is made so that it is easy to attach.

Key quality features

What are the critical sales features? On a shirt they may be the collar points and the back inside neck, which are prominently displayed in the pack, but only one of which is important in wear. What other features are important in wear, like the fit of the collar and its degree of stiffness?

What are the danger points where the desired quality approaches the known quality level of the plant? What action can be taken to raise it where required?

What are the acceptable tolerances?

What trimmings conform to the standards required?

What will be the effect of special processes on the fabric? Some fabrics must be cut to allow for deformation in the fusing presses.

Cloth and trimmings

Cloth inspection

This is vital and, in most cases, should take place as soon as possible after delivery. This will permit speedy corrective action at the supplier's plant. When interest rates rise, cloth stocks and work in process are generally reduced in most companies. Faults discovered at the spreading stage or during manufacture may cause unacceptable delays in delivery and will almost certainly cause efficiency-killing disruption to the production plan.

Cloth inspection is best done on special machines, equipped with unrolling and rerolling facilities, which have speeds which are controllable by the examiner. For some fabrics slack feeding to the reroller is necessary, in order to avoid problems later due to relaxation after laying. A length metering device is standard and at little extra cost the width of the fabric can be monitored to see if it is outside of tolerance. In addition to surface examination, it pays to examine some fabrics by means of underlighting and provision can be made for this.

Testing

Suppliers can be required to enclose a test report from an independent textile testing house and in some cases it pays to have fabric checked independently in the supplier's own premises. At this stage the appropriate care label should be selected but it must cater for all the materials used. Machine washability can often be a key point in sales. Some of the qualities for which it is routine to test are set out below.

Dry clean and washability for dimensional stability, colour fastness and delamination of fusibles.
Colour for match and resistance to fading, especially with respect to ultra-violet light and sulphur compounds.
Abrasion resistance, including colour change.
Pilling, especially for fabrics of mixed fibres.
Bow and skew – a ruler and set square are often enough.
Drape and crease-resistance, including 'permanent press' capability.
Strength – tensile, tear and bursting (for seams).
Flammability, which should be carried out after a set number of washings, etc. in some cases.
Surface wetting and penetration.

Purchasing

The procedure for attaching a cutting of the required cloth should be extended to trimmings. The use of an organisation such as the British Textile Technology Group (BTTG) is not expensive and they will supply a suitable form of contract as well as acting as an independent arbiter. In any case, quality specifications should be set out clearly:

Dimensions of materials, together with the permitted tolerances. These should include the dimensions with respect to weight and thickness, as well as length and width.
Coatings, especially with respect to thickness and degree of penetration, freedom from surface flaws and finish.
Number and type of faults allowed per unit with procedures and allowances in the case of an excessive number of faults.
The system of fault identification, test procedures and arbiter in case of dispute.

Details of the required performance and construction, based on a sample test preport.

Inspection methods

On reception, cloth should be inspected for visible damage and weighed. Net weight gives the yardage if a circular calculator is used. It should be fully examined as soon as possible afterwards, before it goes into store. The minimal equipment required should have two powered rollers, with the speed controlled by the examiner. A metering device checks for length and, at a little extra cost the width can be monitored to see that it is within tolerance. For many fabrics tension-free rerolling is useful in order to avoid problems with relaxation after it is laid up. Apart from good toplights it may also be necessary to cater for underlighting on a second inspection. In any case provision should be made for rerolling printed or surface finished fabrics like velvet.

If provision is made for specified tests in the contract, these may be applied on statistically selected samples. With respect to certain qualities, such as colour, it may be necessary to provide three samples: one as near as possible to that required and two which represent the limits of what is acceptable. Master samples should be stored so that they do not deteriorate. For example, colour masters should be kept free from contamination in a dark place.

In some circumstances it may be helpful to install rail-mounted knives on the machine, in order to cater for the removal of defects. In this case the roll should be marked with strings, in order to assist the people who have to lay up.

Storage

Cloth stocks should be stored so as to avoid soiling or mechanical damage, where possible at a standard temperature and humidity, so that dimensional changes do not take place in store and there is no danger of fungal attack. The ends of rolls must be protected against the light and dirt if stocks are held for any length of time. Care must be taken to avoid distortion or damage during handling. Since most cloth arrives in heavy bolts, mechanical handling not only reduces labour costs but may also avoid damage as well.

Never store cloth directly on the floor or cross stack. Racking, with fabric identification, improves access and reduces damage. Folding into cuttle must only be done one or two days before laying up.

Treatment

Stentering for accurate width and preshrinking may be carried out at this stage. The fusing of lining to some cut parts may also be done in the cloth store and recutting to true dimensions may be necessary. Alternatively, if shrink characteristics are known and consistent, the patterns may be *designed* to the correct oversize and sampling checks for consistent shrinkage carried out. Colour changes can also occur at fusing temperatures or if fusing temperatures are not controlled within the prescribed limits.

Fusibles

The techniques of fusing are relatively new in the industry and are still developing. The subject is, in any case, more complex than can be adequately covered in this book. However, bodies such as the British Interlining Manufacturers Association provide excellent up-to-date information and the representatives of the manufacturers should always be consulted with respect to their products. Set out below are some general guidelines which indicate the main ways in which the quality of the fusing process can be maintained.

Fusing presses

Routine procedures for maintaining the quality of the fusing process are concerned with two types of press. The 'flat-bed' which may also be used for other pressing operations, provides a high labour cost solution, because of its intermittent feed. The continuous process consists of a conveyor belt, which feeds the parts through the heated press heads. The first step is to establish a book in which is recorded all maintenance and the results of all testing, particularly the routine. The press will usually be calibrated after installation and at regular intervals by the suppliers. In addition, regular daily tests should be performed by the press staff. Presses will need to be switched on about an hour before the start of work, unless the makers specify otherwise. The settings of the thermostats should be checked at this stage against the setting cards displayed on the press.

Testing procedures

Tests for temperature may be made with single wire pyrometers, left for at least 20 seconds on flat-bed presses. They may not be used on continuous presses, since they may damage the belts. Thermopapers are permissible for both but record only the maximum temperature. Variations from standard temperature of ±5°C are acceptable but ±2°C is preferred. Checks for temperature should commence 40 minutes after the press has been switched on. First check that the thermostat settings are correct. Do each test twice.

'Flat-beds' should be operated for 6 cycles, 20 seconds open and 20 closed, then the strips of Thermopaper or pyrometer wires should be placed to cover the space symmetrically around the sides, three to each.

Six cycles are necessary whenever the press has been out of use for periods of five minutes or longer and so they should not be switched off during the day.

Continuous presses must be run for 10 minutes before testing and so they too are best left in operation until the end of the day. Four papers, set symmetrically across the width are normally enough.

Testing routines

Temperature tests are necessary at the start of the shift and after every break in production and should total at least three times a day.

Testing for pressure can be done on a weekly basis. First check that the pressure setting is correct for the fusible in use. Pressure should be monitored by the operative during the day in case it falls off.

For 'flat-beds' place brown paper strips, each 5 cms wide along the edges in the places used for temperature testing. When the press is closed they should be held firmly. After this check that the press cladding is in order.

The continuous press is tested in a similar way. Strips of paper are fed under the nip rollers and the press is stopped. Then each is pulled firmly. Bowing is the main problem with this type of press and so the centre requires particular attention.

Timing should the checked against a stopwatch daily.

Peel strength tests must be carried out twice daily or following a major change of fabric. This is done by making up test pieces of fabric and fusible, selecting those which are most likely to give trouble. For large parts a strip 5 cms wide is necessary but 2.5 cms is enough for small parts. The lengh should be 1.5 cms along the weft direction. When cool they may be pulled apart using a spring gauge, a job which requires a little skill if it is to be done consistently. Three or four strips across the width of the press are recommended. The first should be done about ten minutes after the start of production.

All test results must be entered into a special book at once, entries being made on dated pages which record the date and time, together with details of any problems encountered and of any maintenance work.

Cutting

Precision

Accurate control of cloth width produces economies in edge margins. Precise cutting not only avoids spoilt work at the making up stage but is the key to modern sewing room practice – 'fitting up' and 'lining trimming' should be regarded as redundant operations. Net cutting, an essential part of garment engineering, demands precision in cutting and low shape deformation afterwards.

Laying up

Inspect all cloth during laying up if it has not been done previously. In any case, with modern laying up machines it should be easy to check the previous examination in the cloth store. A mirror suspended over the table will permit a full coverage of the cloth width. Some fabrics must be allowed to relax before cutting but spreaders with a slack feed can do much to reduce difficulties because of this. Where storage conditions are humid, steps must be taken to dry the cloth fully before laying up or before cutting.

The main faults, which are to be avoided during this stage, are poor edge alignment and stretched cloth. Of course, only one edge can be aligned and it is on this that the cutter's attention is focussed in manual laying. As a result it is easy for major defects in the cloth to be missed. It is always better to use a slack feed if there is any danger of the cloth stretching during the lay. Even so, it is necessary with some cloths to allow time for 'relaxation' after laying and before cutting. This ties up expensive cutting tables and is to be avoided if possible. Tests on a new cloth on receipt may save money later.

Other faults are: fabric spread too loosely; plies not spread as planned, one way or alternatively; spread distortion due to static electricity and the mismatch of patterns, particularly checks. The last can be avoided by the use of hanging tables, check spikes or by cutting singles, all of which tend to be labour-consuming, although computer cutting of singles does reduce the labour cost.

Marking in

Two main types are in use. In one a new lay is drawn each time. This has the advantage that any new patterns will be automatically included. However, it is not considered to be economically feasible to check each one for error. In the second a master may be prepared. In this case it is usually best to check them. The separation between patterns should vary between lays, to allow for the deviation of the cutting knife, so that lays with many plies, plies of thicker material or of a weave which tends to deflect the knife should have a wider separation. This is not possible if a standard laymarker is used in each case. The widest separation will give the required accuracy at the expense of cloth utilisation. Marking directly onto the cloth avoids error due to the pattern slipping. Several methods are available:

Chalk. The traditional method, direct to the cloth. The lines are thick.
Perforated markers. A master is made from waxed paper and the pattern marked in by perforations. The top ply is marked directly by powdered chalk, which does not give a sharp line.
Spray marking. The patterns are laid on to the top ply and the lay

sprayed. The parts to be used are left unsprayed. Errors arise due to paint build up on the patterns.

Pencil markers. These give sharp, easily seen lines on paper.

Carbon markers. Only a limited number of carbon markers will have sharp lines.

Photo markers. Full-scale patterns are laid up and the results photographed for future use. Accurate and, with a suitable shade contrast, easy to read but expensive.

Spirit duplicators. This is a wet process and shrinkage, especially with the cheaper papers, is a problem. There is a limit to the number of clear markers which can be made.

Computer markers. Masters can be stored in the usual magnetic media, such as floppy discs. The print out is always sharp and easy to read. Separation can be varied in some versions. New patterns for parts of the lay can be introduced without difficulty. Some automatic checking is possible.

Cutting

Accurate cutting saves money. Most cutting rooms pay insufficient attention to this fact. Little of the expertise in the training for manual skills found in modern sewing rooms has spilled over into the cutting room, where day release is the only gesture in that direction. College training concentrates on the considerable amount of job knowledge required for even the craft qualifications.

There appears to be little evidence to support the practice of allowing a substantial separation between patterns in the laymarker and it is often possible to reduce these for most depths of lay and most types of fabric. The secret is a very limited amount of investigation and good management to insist that quality standards are met. A survey by the British Clothing Centre in 1985 proposed that separation be eliminated, between large parts and where die cutting is used, for elastic fabrics in the foundation garment industry.

Powered tools

Round knives
These consist of a cutting disc supported by a rail or stand. Their main use is for straight cuts for splicing or end cutting, where the gyroscopic action of the blade is useful in maintaining the line. Rail mounting ensures a cut at right angles to the edge of the lay for these purposes.

Straight knives
A reciprocating blade and motor is mounted on a stand which runs on the table top, usually on wheels but occasionally on an air cushion. Their application is in the separation of blocks for the band knife or for cutting

out parts from the lay. Computerised cutters usually make use of a cantilever arm to support the straight knife. Even for manual work such a system offers advantages, because of reduced friction, fabric distortion and operative fatigue.

Band knives

This is the original form of powered knife. It requires more manual skill to use than a straight knife but is more dangerous. Its nature permits the use of a narrower and more flexible blade than that of the straight knife, which is helpful in cutting out detail. It does not have the tendency to cut short at the bottom of the lay, which occurs with the straight knife, due to wear.

The main distortions come from movement of the plies during the movement of blocks onto the cutting table.

Drills

Easily seen drill holes are a helpful guide to the positioning of such items as pockets in the sewing room. They are not generally suitable for knitted fabrics.

Plain types are often sufficient for close weaves.

Gouging points cut out a disc and are more easily seen in thick, loose weaves.

Hypodermic types release a dye as they are withdrawn. With suitable ball points they are unlikely to cause runs in knits, since the threads need not be cut for the purpose of marking. Preferably they should be covered during garment construction, like the other drill holes but the use of fluorescent and volatile dyes (driven off during pressing) permits wider application.

The following table summarises the problems of powered knives and how to rectify them.

Device	Defect	Cures
All powered knives	Most	Training in manual skills.
	Fused edges, frayed edges and scorching	Slower cutting speeds, sharp blades, special blades (notched or wavy and/or striated), antifusion paper and blade cooling by volatile non-staining fluid (compressed air is expensive and disturbs the lay).
Straight knives	Failure to follow marker	Marker positioned correctly and secure; lighter, slower machines; better clamping/vacuum and air cushion mounting.

Device	Defect	Cures
"	"	Table width should be greater than that of the laymarker by at least twice the length of the base of the knife.
"	Cut out of vertical	Proper table width; heavier machine base; horizontal table and replacement of worn blades.
Band knives	Failure to follow marker	Marker positioned correctly and secure; air flotation cutting table; better clamping and smaller blocks. Pull cutting gives better vision but is more dangerous. Sliding blocks to trolleys for the movement to the cutting table.*

Note: Pneumatic, adjustable trolleys are cheap to run. The top of the table or the previous block can be adjusted to that of the laying up or cutting table, so that blocks can be slid onto and off the trolleys. Canvas stretched beneath the lay can be rolled in towards the cutting table at the end to serve a similar purpose.

Underlay paper stops the bottom ply from rucking when the base of the powered knife or drill passes beneath it. The glazed side must be underneath.

Interleaving tissue of different colours separates the plies in the lay. If ten garments are required in a bundle it can be laid every tenth ply or it can be used to separate shades.

Antifusion paper, instead of tissue, helps to reduce the fusing of cut edges.

Laymarkers can be secured to the lay by means of weights (which may cause interply movement), staples or by means of heat sealing. Staples, set into waste cloth, are generally the best.

Removing defective cloth

Defects often extend across the weft. They are usually removed by means of two straight cuts at right angles to the edge.

Straight splice
A straight splice is used where there is a break in the pattern of the lay. A 5 cm overlap is added by convention but with rail-mounted circular knives this may be reduced. The underlay paper is marked with a single line.

(a)

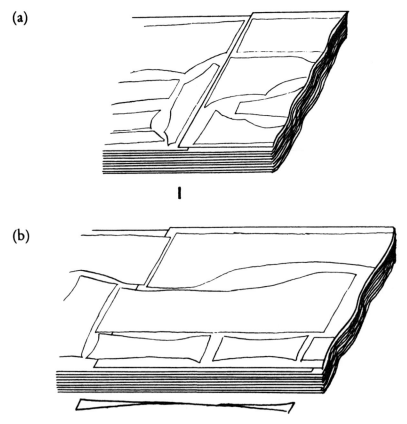

I

(b)

Fig. 9.1 (a) Straight splice. (b) Interlock splice.

Interlock splice
Where the patterns interlock sufficient overlap must be allowed to avoid a pattern piece being cut and with a small margin for error. The spare material is used for recuts unless shading is a problem. The underlay paper is marked on the margin with a line at each end of the splice and diagonals drawn between them.

String
The damage is marked by a string only. When the lay has been cut the faulty part is removed and replaced by a recut. The method is very economical where shading is not a problem.

Cutting's key role

The emphasis given to cutting in 'Total Quality Control' is proportional to the effect on quality which can be achieved in most clothing companies by attention to this department. A little extra work in cutting can save a far greater amount of time in making up and can slash quality costs. A good general rule is to make all notches Vs, since they are easier to see and a partly cut notch is more obvious.

Making up

General principles

The quality control problems in the making up department are tied closely to those for the whole factory. A good basic rule for operatives on incentive payment is that they should not be paid for their own repairs and that a record should be kept of their quality performance. They should do all their own unpicking and repairs. Where this would cause too great an upset to balancing, the incentive scheme may be modified so that time spent by other operatives, floaters and supervisors may be deducted from the standard minutes earned by the offender. If defect levels are held down to their proper level this should cause no hardship. In most factories defect levels are far above this and the responsibility is that of management for failing to spot bad work in time.

Handling

The movement of cut parts around the sewing room should be kept to a minimum; for example, it usually pays to make up parts separately and to deliver them direct to a matching-in point. Most creasing is due to poor handling techniques. Moreover, the more people who handle a garment the more likely are lost parts and soiling.

Quality specifications

The secret is to have simple, well illustrated, factory standards understood by all. Then variations for individual styles are easily communicated. There is often a relation between the volume of paper devoted to specifications and poor quality! Quality specifications must be specific and measurable wherever possible and tolerances are essential. There is a widespread practice whereby standards are set at too high a level 'because operatives always work below them'. Of course they do if poor work is accepted! The subject is discussed in more detail in a later section in this chapter under 'Quality audit'.

Intermediate examination

The purpose of this is to detect bad work before too much is made and before parts in which there are defects are incorporated. With the majority of production systems the examination workplaces are located at physical positions in the line. Once a position is established it is seldom changed.

Although sampling cuts down the work involved and the delays to the flow of garments these are still significant. Some flexibility can be achieved, at the cost of space, by manning the positions on a part-time basis and stepping up the sampling rate when bad work occurs.

Consider a garment made successively on five lines, with a throughput time of three days per line. If an operative at the beginning of the first line began to make poor work it would be fifteen days before it was discovered at final machine examination. Fifteen days' work could by then be defective.

Thus, sufficient intermediate examination positions must be selected and set up in order to yield an adequate detection rate. The criteria for their insertion into the line are as follows:

Minimum defective WIP
This depends upon the work content and the predicted defect levels between intermediate examination positions.

Permanent damage
If bad work cannot be repaired it becomes even more urgent to stop it.

Critical features
Certain parts of a garment such as the collar are critical to its appearance.

Trouble spots
Trainees, operatives on transfer and operations where the quality level is lower than required, are all potential dangers.

Matching in
It is better to put bad work right before joining it to good.

Modern mechanical work movement processes permit examination positions to be sited physically in one place and to deal with work at any stage of its production on that line. This permits a dynamic response to changes in the operations which are generating high defect levels. This results in 'flexible intermediate examination' in which the siting conditions can be met more exactly and reviewed on a weekly basis. Flexibility of a different sort is possible since the examiners for one line can be grouped together. This makes it easier to deal with absenteeism on the part of examiners and fluctuating work loads due to multiple sampling.

Patrol examination

Flexibility of another sort results from the use of this approach. The examiners have no fixed workstation but roam the line checking work as seems appropriate. They may follow the main criteria more easily than with 'fixed intermediate examination' but their discretion may be used wrongly, picking on people that they do not like or checking the work of friends as an excuse for a chat. Bureaucratic rules are clumsy and are often ignored. The best solution is for *supervisors* to do their examination in this way. If they do not have enough time, make their sections smaller. You may need some more supervisors but you will need many fewer examiners.

The causes of seam pucker

Seam pucker is covered in great detail in the booklets issued by the thread manufacturers, which are a mine of information in this and other stitching problems. The following is a summary of possible causes.

Fabric. Closely woven and/or resin-treated fabric has less space for the thread between the threads.
Threads. If threads are too thick they take up too much space.
Stitch density. The more stitches there are the more they pack the fabric.
Seam direction along the weft generally gives the worst results.
Type of seam. Lockstitches interlock within the fabric.
Thread tension should be kept to a minimum to reduce pucker.
Interply slippage causes one ply to be fed faster than the other. With lockstitch drop feed is worst and the cures are puller feed, top and bottom feed, walking feet, teflon-coated or ball feet and best of all – needle feed. With the spread of faster machines and semi-automation the practice by which the operative feeds the top ply forward by hand is becoming increasingly uneconomic.
Differential shrinkage. A mismatch between thread and fabric causes pucker on washing.

Work aids

Properly maintained automatic machinery will normally give a better and more consistent quality than manual methods. However, operatives may require retraining if the greatest advantage is to be taken of it. For example, on the old lockstitch machines it was usual to trap the tail of thread by pulling it to the left and trapping it under the presser foot. With underbed thread trimmers the tail must be left in the line of sew.

Edge margins
Compensating feet, different widths of presser foot, edge guides, graduated needle plates, and (for temporary use) strips of coloured insulating tape on the needle plate.
   Jigs give margins which are automatically correct.

Fullness
In theory notches may be provided which must be matched to give the correct fullness in, say, sleeve setting. In practice, experienced machinists

will not bother because it slows them down. Automatic machines are faster, more reliable and require less training for the operatives.

Positioning
Prepress, jig stitching and positioning by drill holes or notches are all necessary for cheap, consistent quality patch pockets. For other items spot welds, fusible staples and tape can help with some problems. Blind stitch tackers are an expensive alternative.

Folders and hemmers
Traditionally, stainless steel is the material for binders and 'hemmers. White metal and even polystyrene card are quicker to form and can provide a factory-produced alternative for shorter runs.

Operative comfort
The fundamental work aid. Adjustable chairs with lumbar support are essential. Sometimes raising a work table on blocks for a tall operative can have dramatic results.

Pressing

The best way to a crease-free garment is to crease it as little as possible during manufacture.

Underpressing
This is useful for opening seams and some minor fusing. It should be kept to a minimum.

Moulding
This is a method by which three-dimensional shapes are produced from fabric without the aid of darts. It can be utilised to correct poor sewing but too often this becomes the norm.
   Die presses can be useful for collars.
   Unwanted shrinkage will occur if dwelling times and/or temperatures are too high. Vital chemicals may be evaporated from plastics so that they become brittle.

Steam tunnels
For many garments and fabrics, if creasing is kept to a minimum these, together with a little touch-up pressing, may be all that is necessary.

Form presses
A form of light moulding, these are for problems which cannot be solved by tunnels. Often they are combined with automatic touch-up pressing.

Heads and bucks
Even trained operatives may cheat to speed throughput. Automatic operation is the best approach.

Three-dimensional presses must give better results, especially for key areas such as the foreparts, collars and shoulders. Carousel set ups reduce the labour content.

The right cladding is essential to good quality. It protects the surface, distributing steam and pressure evenly, and allows vacuum to operate effectively. High local steam or physical pressure causes shine on some fabrics, especially synthetics, which it is difficult or impossible to remove. Steam and physical pressure must be kept to a minimum. A cladding designed for low pressures cannot function properly at high ones. Head vacuum helps to avoid impressions from linings etc. with some lightweight and high pile fabrics.

Air blown from the buck serves a similar purpose.

Traditionally, these presses hinge down. A final closing in a vertical plane makes sure that the surfaces are parallel and helps when head vacuum and blowing are applied.

Shrinkage

Ths should not occur unless planned. If it does then the fabric and/or the process is wrong.

After make

Quality audit

Involvement by management is demonstrated if the senior production staff carry out a quality audit (other than an audit under ISO 9000) daily and all the other senior members of management do so at least once a month. The increase in involvement on the part of non-production staff is often dramatic. Even members of the production team may find that it gives them a new insight.

A quality audit (see Fig. 9.2) may consist of the examination of as few as ten finished garments. Where possible these should be of styles which are representative of current throughput, although specialists, such as designers, may wish to pay particular attention to one style. Scoring should be of the form set out below.

Critical	5	Requires replacement or extensive rework.
Serious	3	Repairs or sale as a 'second' recommended.
Noticeable	2	Only minor rectification needed. (Thread ends and minor creasing are examples.)
Minor	1	Within tolerance but outside of control limits. (Such a defect as would not normally call for rejection unless there were several.)

Opn. No.	Defect Description	Garments →	1	2	3	4	5	6	7	8	9	10
	TOTAL											

Examined by _____ _____   Date _____ ____

Fig. 9.2 Sample garment quality audit form.

Systematic examination

Standard procedures for the examination of typical garments are a vital part of quality control. They make sure that all the features of the garment are covered and attention directed to the key points. These procedures are also labour-saving and are particularly useful for people who do not usually do this work, like the managers mentioned above. Readers may note that not all of the routes are mentioned on the example given. These would be included in a separate size and measurement chart.

An example of an examiner's guide is given in Fig. 9.3.

Customer returns

Very often the quality level is set by buyers for the shops that sell the merchandise. Commonly this standard does not correspond to what the ultimate customer wants. Analysis of genuine customer returns may often permit a relaxation of some specifications and make it possible to reduce the price slightly. The quality audit form is used for this purpose but with an extra category added: 'other' for returns which are accepted for customer goodwill but which fall within the quality specifications.

Department *Menswear*	Date Installed. 1.1.95
Garment/Style *All jackets*	Size Range *all*
Operation *All to final machine pass*	*JACKET FRONT*

EXAMINATION PROCEDURES	KEY POINTS
1 & 4 Shoulders	*Smooth lines*
2 & 5 Sleeves	*Set correctly, no peaking on front drape, fullness over shoulder*
3 & 6 Cuffs	*Buttons correct type & secure.*
7 & 10 Collar	*Sits square on jacket, leaf edge clean, points sharp.*
8 & 11 Lapels	*Rolled & not creased, turnover at break.*
9 & 12 Front edges	*Seam edge visible only at break. Buttons & holes coincide.*
18 Front hem	*Level.*

Fig. 9.3 Example of an examiner's guide.

Sealed samples

These are actual garments which are a convenient way of recording what the bulk buyer wants.

Check examining

This is done by the senior examiner or a specially appointed and senior examiner. The procedure is much the same as for the quality audit, and is really a form of the same thing. A good final examiner may miss from 10 to 15 per cent of the defects in a batch of garments.

The quality cycle

(1) Find out what is the required quality at what price and what volume.
(2) Is the required quality at or below the factory quality level?
(3) Accept the order if it is at the Factory Quality Level (FQL) or below. Reject it if the standard required is above the FQL or negotiate a reduced level.
(4) Will it make an acceptable profit?
(5) Design to suit the market requirements.
(6) Draw up a quality specification.
(7) Make it.
(8) *Sales staff sell what the factory makes at the required volume and price.* Mere order takers do not.

10

Production and People

Introduction

Production is only partly programmable

Most technical jobs can be done successfully once a routine has been established. Routine is vital to a good production manager, if only to reduce the number of emergencies. Nevertheless, emergencies always occur in manufacturing, because it is manufacturing which employs most of the people, particularly in our industry. This chapter concentrates on the way that supervisors can best use the talents of the people who make up their sections.

Perfection

It has been written that good supervisors should:

- know all the techniques of their job;
- understand and be conversant with all company policies;
- arrive at work before their staff and leave after them;
- prepare for the following day before going home;
- be skilled in all the jobs on their section;
- understand and be able to adjust all the machines;
- be loyal, courteous, well dressed, enthusiastic, healthy, patient, energetic, a good teacher, respected and liked by all.

Reality

Management are looking for supervisors, not super-supervisors. The perfection outlined above is a fine target and good supervisors will possess all of the qualities to some degree but will be bound to have their own set of strengths and weakness.

If supervisors can induce amongst their staff a spirit of willing co-operation, coupled with an enthusiastic interest in quality and productivity, they will have most of the virtues required.

The effective use of human resources is the aspect of supervision which is covered in this chapter.

Effective control of a group depends upon an understanding of how it works and how it will choose its leader. Managers appoint supervisors but groups appoint leaders.

Good *communication* is essential. The most important aspect of good communication is that it is a two-way street. Listening can be more important than talking. Keeping the section well-informed is one of the best ways of establishing leadership.

Discipline is the cement that holds a group together, in order to fulfil its purpose, and is consequently closely tied to its morale. A group without a purpose ceases to be a group.

A basic guide to supervising people

Example and honesty

In any group of people, most will attempt to model themselves on their leader and so it is essential for supervisors to set a good example. Ideally they should know all the aspects of the job thoroughly. If they do not know something they should be open about this, showing honesty and keenness to learn by asking questions of the mechanics etc. in front of their operatives.

When things go wrong they should try to be calm and cheerful, shouldering the responsibility.

Thinking like a supervisor

Think ahead
Plan systematically and carry through the plan in a thorough manner. People like to work in a smoothly run organisation.

Welcome change
Changes cause occasional upheavals but are essential to survival in today's competitive world.

Supervise
This is what you are paid to do. Time spent at a machine, doing work which your operatives should do, like repairs, means that you have not got time to do your proper job, such as preventing poor work.

Discipline

Rules
Make sure that you understand the rules and then insist that your operatives obey them.

Firmness
Never turn a blind eye to trouble but deal with infringements as they occur and always see that the blame for error rests where it belongs, even with yourself, if that is correct.

Stages of discipline
Be pleasant, but firm when dealing with slackness. If your own efforts fail, take the offender to management but make sure of your facts first.

Courtesy

Friendly but firm
You will be much more effective if people like to work for you. Try to be equally pleasant and friendly with all of your operatives. Some will be more co-operative than others and it may be tempting or even fair to favour them occasionally but do not do it.

Even handedness
Try to give every operative the same amount of attention and the same opportunity to learn.

Courtesy
Give praise where it is due; always say please and thank you.

> Influencing friends is easy – influencing enemies is not.

Communication

Teamwork
Keep people informed, since they will not feel part of something unless they have a good idea of what that something is and how it works. One way to give your team more interest and satisfaction in their job is to make them understand the vital role that they play in their company and to make them feel part of a thriving group.

Integration
Make sure that they know how their job affects other people. Inform them about overall company news and policy (changes in management,

new styles etc.). Pass on any nice remarks about quality or output made by higher management. When a company executive pays a visit, make sure that the team know who it is and, if possible, get the visitor to talk to them, speaking of any of their recent achievements.

Loyalty and rivalry

Integrity
Never, in the presence of your section, make disparaging remarks about other supervisors or managers. Never pass the buck up or down. Stand up for your section and protect their earnings when representing them. Do not court popularity by blaming management for everything that your operatives dislike.

Competition
Friendly rivalry between sections and individuals is a good thing, since it helps production and promotes interest. Serious rivalry can be disastrous.

The rewards of supervision

Supervising even a small unit can be an enormously demanding and, at times, frustrating job. The reward is the satisfaction which comes from overcoming its technical difficulties and even more from the development of your own personality, to fulfil the vital role of motivating and guiding others. And you have got to enjoy that.

> Control events – do not let them control you.

Leading groups of people

Understanding the group
The success or failure of a supervisor depends to a very large extent on maintaining good relations with the workforce. To do this the supervisor must understand them thoroughly as a group and as individuals.

This chapter is based on sound academic research but that does not mean that supervisors must concentrate on learning all about psychology and sociology. On the contrary, given the guidelines which we shall discuss, their strength lies in their practical knowlede of their workforce. They will not be expected to apply the principles blindly but in the light of their own assessment of the many local factors involved.

> Efficient control depends upon understanding.

Groups exist for a purpose

However much people enjoy each other's company they do not, in general, form a group except for a set purpose. The locals at the pub have their darts team, the Mother's Union their lectures, and the section at work is primarily intended to produce parts of garments.

Leaders

Leaders are produced by groups. The old idea of the 'natural leader' has now been discarded and it is recognised that different groups of people and different situations will cause different types of people to emerge as leaders.

One group may have more than one sort of leader: in the family, father may make the decision about the sort of car to buy whereas mother might pick the curtains. Leaders generally represent the aspirations of the group.

The leader of a group is generally well thought of by his or her followers because he or she possesses special skills and/or is popular.

Group spirit

People who have much to do with each other soon form bonds of affection. It is a commonplace that a family busy squabbling amongst themselves will unite if one of their number is threatened by an outsider. The group spirit of the fan club or the followers of a local football team is also well known.

> Groups make leaders.

Prestige within in group

The achievement of true prestige is important to a supervisor in order to be the real as well as the nominal leader of the section. The most important motivation for some of their operatives may be prestige.

The group usually expects its members to conform, often in matters of dress. Certainly some sort of uniform is often adopted by even the most informal groups – witness the 'punks'.

The good sportswoman will be heard with deference in the tennis club, the soloist in the choir and the excellent pieceworker in the clothing factory.

A bore is someone who talks about himself when we wish to talk about ourselves. The good listener is assured of a place in any group.

Authority and respect

We all resent being told what to do, although this reaction may be tempered by a lazy inclination to leave decisions to someone else. Leaders reduce their popularity by the extent to which they seem to assert their authority. Of course tact may reduce the appearance of authority and group effectiveness under their leadership will enhance their prestige. An individual may not choose to leave a voluntary group, even though disliking the leader, but if enough people resent the authority of the leader they will choose another, even in a formal industrial environment.

> Identify group ideals.

Individuals

Prestige seekers
Nominally many people work hard at boring jobs for money. The real answer may be that they enjoy the prestige of being a top pieceworker. Then public praise from the supervisor may be very effective.

Conformists
Other people may work at a factory because they like it there, failing to achieve high output because of lack of effort or skill but rarely falling below 80 BSI. Their lack of achievement may be because they are frightened that they will stand out. They may say that they do not wish to 'show off'. Here an appeal to team spirit will often work wonders.

Rebels
Some people have a drive to defy authority and are often known as 'trouble makers'. Frequently they can be converted to prestige seekers but it is important to impose formal authority as little as possible.

Others
The list is endless for no two people are alike. Nevertheless they will all work best if treated as individuals but as individuals who belong to a group.

Effective supervision

The old-fashioned supervisor wanted production at all costs. More recently the emphasis has been on sweetness and light as a reaction against this, with the implication that a happy work force was more important than output. Effective supervision places due emphasis on good human relations as part of a balanced approach intended to secure the greatest efficiency. People who are unhappy at work are more inclined to absenteeism and to be less co-operative. Hard work, as part of an efficient team, can be very satisfying although it would be foolish to pretend that good wages are not the main reason why people work, especially where there is a sensible and simple incentive scheme.

Communication

Supervision is impossible without adequate communication. One American expert has estimated that commununication takes up 80 per cent of the time of a supervisor. It may conveniently be divided into three categories:

- management policies and employee reaction;
- directives and plans relating to production requirements;
- operating detail.

Management policies and employee reactions

Good management will keep workers informed of all that is likely to affect them and will take note of the employees' reaction, acting on it if possible. The supervisor is the channel through which this communication must pass. Done badly this can result in an 'us and them' attitude; done well it can result in a closely knit team with a common purpose.

Supervisors should speak of 'our policy' and 'this is what we are going to do'. Written handouts from the manager can be a useful back-up sometimes, but they are only a form of one-way communication. Interpretation, explanation and a readiness to pass comment back up the line are essential. Nevertheless before passing on the reaction of an individual a supervisor should check on the reactions of the rest of the staff. If based on an isolated comment it must be described as such and not made to appear as a general one. Never should a reaction be exaggerated.

Production requirements

As far as possible this should form part of a routine:

- daily production estimates;
- hourly balancing rounds;
- routine completion of other records such as training curve graphs.

Receiving instructions
Listen to the person giving the instruction and pick out the key details. Afterwards report back what you believe you are to do. If a discussion follows, re-summarise and check again, using examples if there is any doubt. Beware of bosses who 'discuss' things in a vague way. If things go wrong they may then say that you have misunderstood. In such cases a

written summary may be necessary and it should be read back to make sure that there is no doubt.

Giving instructions

Here you are more in control of the situation. Ensure that your subordinate follows the procedure outlined above. You will need to think out your plan in advance, as far as possible, since if a number of alternatives are discussed it may be difficult to remember which was the one agreed.

- Plan and note key points including deadlines.
- Explain your intentions and (briefly) the reasons.
- Inform in stages using sketches if necessary.
- Recapitulate the key points after each stage.
- Listen to your subordinates' version of each stage.
- Discuss examples.
- Summarise and check again if the session lasts longer than a few minutes.

> Engage brain before opening mouth.

Notebooks

A notebook beats any memory. Rule a margin down the left hand side and put in the initials of the person to whom you are to speak. Write the key points in the other space.

- Think.
- Record.
- Inform the person responsible and date the entry.
- Check that the work has been carried out as agreed and cross out the entry.

Cross-communication

- Does the instruction affect others?
- How will they be informed?
- What are the approved channels?
- Note all who have to be informed and check that this has been done.

Beware of the person who thinks that it is possible to listen whilst busy with something else. Stand and wait until you have the person's full attention.

Before you communicate you must establish contact. A remark on a new hairstyle and you have your hearer's attention – then you communicate. Too often the first part of a message is lost whilst the recipient 'tunes in'.

Plan.
Inform.
Check.
Correct.

Discipline

The meaning of discipline

Discipline means different things to different people. In this book it is defined as 'the body of rules, formal and informal, which govern the conduct of a group and the reason that those rules are obeyed'. We shall consider how supervisors can work within the framework which exists in the factory; how they can improve the aims of their groups (the sections) so that they fall into line with the objectives of the company.

> Be hard on yourself but lenient with others.

A profitable company, producing a high volume of good quality clothes at a reasonable cost, is a sensible aim for everyone. It will provide secure employment and sufficient profits to permit good wages, decent working conditions and investment in the future. A legitimate secondary aim for the 'pieceworker' is high bonus earnings and for the supervisor promotion and job satisfaction.

Correcting faults

The blasting for someone who produces bad work is an old-fashioned approach. Nevertheless, however enlightened our views, people will occasionally break the rules and spoil the team's effort. Then their work-mates will expect the supervisor to take action. A positive approach will prevent this occuring too often. Some examples of fault and how to deal with them are set out below.

Low quality
Jeanette is a hard worker, keen to earn a high bonus but her quality is poor. First analyse the reason for this.

- Are the machine and workplace in order?
- Is the quality level achievable?

- Is her skill adequate?
- Has there been too much speed or carelessness?

If the poor quality is her fault, then motivate her to want to do better. One way is to ensure that she does her own repairs and so loses money by her slackness. Another might be to discuss the problem with her, so that she realises the effect that her bad work has. Her fellow operatives may help with this if their workflow is interrupted. The final step is to offer assistance to improve.

Analyse.   Motivate.   Help.

Low output
Mary works well below her capacity but her quality is excellent. Apart from the approach outlined above, a capacity check and the setting of hourly goals is often the path to success. If the method is wrong some coaching will be necessary and a video is often the key to swift improvement. Sometimes such people are better suited to hourly paid work, such as repairs or examining, although speed is important to examiners too. Sometimes the low output is new. The fall-off in performance may be due to a variety of causes from the need for spectacles to an unhappy love affair.

Personal cleanliness
Joan smells. If she has close friends they may be able to help but beware the girl who starts her conversation with 'The supervisor says you smell!' Tact and the support of the group are the best aids.

Fighting
If operatives fight do not separate them yourself but, if you can, get their friends to do so. Keep them separate and do your best to reduce the tension. At all costs avoid taking sides and keep your own involvement to a minimum whilst tempers are high. In most factories suspension is automatic for such an offence. Once the offenders are out of the way it is always advisable to obtain statements from any witnesses and the manager must be informed as soon as possible.

Be fair and friendly but firm.

Disciplinary procedures
Many countries now have a legal requirement for proper disciplinary procedures. These are, in any case, of value both to both employer and employees. Good supervisors know what is laid down for their factory and stick to the rules.

Maintaining morale

Be a good listener
A friendly 'shoulder to cry on' pays back in two ways, you reinforce your position as leader and you keep yourself informed as to what is happening in your section.

Team spirit
Encourage the group feeling: friendly rivalry with other sections is generally a good thing. 'We never keep other sections waiting' is the form. Occasional outings as a group are desirable, though not always possible.

Jokes
A friendly atmosphere is a great aid to production and an occasional joke; a little chat should be encouraged. Do your best to make your operatives want to come to work but remember that they are there to sew and not to skylark.

Confidence
Your operatives must have confidence in you. Make decisions when they are necessary, anticipate problems, stick up for your staff when it is right to do so and you will command their confidence.

Dignity
It is easier to define what dignity is not, rather than what it is. It is *not*:

- screaming at workers who do wrong;
- playing practical jokes on your staff;
- dressing in an unbecoming way.

Nevertheless, some supervisors can do the most outrageous things and retain the respect of their staff. The secret lies in the supervisor and the operatives, and what they regard as natural behaviour.

> Dignity is not pomposity.

Complaints and requests

Stock complaints
These form a fairly long list but it is worthwhile to make one out for your section and to think out the replies in advance.

'I always get the awkward jobs.'
'The mechanic always keeps me waiting when my machine breaks down.'
'The water in the toilets is too hot/cold.'
'Mary was rude to me.'

Stock requests
Some, like complaints, are merely calls for attention, whilst others, also like some complaints, are excuses for poor work. Some may be dealt with at once and others require consultation with managers and/or other supervisors.

Correct approach
Always listen courteously and try to avoid an argument ('I see your point'). Never fail to answer a complaint or a query as soon as possible.

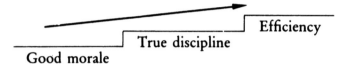

Efficiency

True discipline

Good morale

11

Training

Introduction

How people learn

Learning is a process of widening our skills and our awareness by stepping out from what we know already. People must want to learn if it is to be done effectively. The more active the involvement of the trainees, the more quickly they will learn. Once something is learned, the new skill must be firmly established before a new one is attempted. The traditional method, by which people helped out here and there, until settling into their own job, is exactly the wrong method. Often skilled workers are unaware of the special way in which they achieve results. The difference between an expert and a trainee is usually the way in which the expert is always looking forward to the next step.

Putting training to work

Training at all levels requires the same basic steps:

- Establish what is to be taught.
- Plan the training sequence.
- Prepare each lesson.
- Show and tell what is to be learnt.
- Let the trainee practise.
- Praise what is right and gently correct what is wrong.
- Compare the performance with established standards.
- Follow up.

Leadership training

Like any practical skill, leadership can be learned but it is difficult to teach. To some extent it requires changes of attitude and a system is described by which supervisors can be trained away from their sections. It is based upon the anonymous comment of fellow trainees, which is far more effective than advice from an 'expert'.

How people learn

Learning

Learning is a process by which we extend our knowledge and skills, using the information given to us by our senses. We learn far more easily when we truly wish to do so, and part of the problem of good instruction is the provision of satisfactory motivation.

The senses

- Sight.
- Hearing.
- Touch. } Memory plays a part with all.
- Taste.
- Smell.

Kinaesthesia

This is the sixth sense: the one that tells you how tightly you are grasping cloth when you feed it to the machine; that guides your hand to the back tack lever, when your eyes are looking at the work being sewn. It has been described as an internal sense of touch.

Using the senses in training

We learn best by *DOING*, next by *seeing* and worst by *listening*. A good instructor uses the senses together and gives the trainee a chance to practise as soon as this is possible, without the trainee becoming discouraged by failure or having a high risk of injury.

Step by step

In general we learn by building on what we know. Small steps mean a greater chance that the instruction can be short and the practice successful. Someone who has learned to recognise figures by adding and subtracting on paper will be much quicker to learn to do so on a calculator than someone who is starting from scratch. There can be problems when the process involves some unlearning. If you know how to drive using an automatic gearbox, you will need to unlearn some of your old habits but you will still do better than a beginner. When constructing the steps it is as well to try to avoid any unnecessary unlearning.

Skills are more difficult to learn than we remember

To the skilled even complicated jobs are easy. Often we forget how bewildering it was when we were learning and underestimate the problems of instruction, rushing it as a result. To someone from school the very factory itself, with its noise and bustle, may be tiring and distracting.

Job knowledge

Part of the skill of every job consists of knowledge. The operatives must know how their machines work, how to carry out simple maintenance and who to call when they have a serious problem. They must know how work comes to them and what they must do with it when the operation is finished. The procedures for bundle handling, quality specification and tolerances are all vital. Most important of all is the sequence of operations for their specialist job. Job knowledge is often neglected in the training plan for operatives. It needs special techniques to teach it and must not be left as an incidental to training in manual dexterity.

Manual dexterity

The practical skills associated with most operative and craft jobs are called this to distinguish them from the job knowledge aspects. They are often also called 'job skills'. The training must be designed to establish patterns of movement which become instinctive and where the eyes are looking forward to the next task for most of the time, leaving 'kinaesthesia' to guide the hands. Each change of the pattern of movement is being triggered by something the operative sees, feels in the muscles, hears or even smells; there are no delays (for routine operations) whilst the next step is thought through. The best analogy is the daily drive to work by an experienced motorist. If all goes well the motorist may remember nothing of the journey but, if a child steps off the pavement in front of the car, a swerve or a jab on the brakes occurs before the fact has registered with the driver.

Anticipation

It is worth repeating that the key to skilled performance is a detailed subconscious knowledge of the work sequence, which includes the location of parts, tools and machine controls. Being able to do the work 'blindfold' is not such an exaggeration as it sounds. For a top performer, planning the next part of the operation takes place during the preceding movement. Beginners deal with each move and manipulation separately.

Skill transfer

It is easier to take a small step in learning than a big one, as we have already established. This applies to retraining too. A person who is used to sewing a 30 cm seam will quickly learn to do similar seams which are 45 cm long. It will take longer for someone who is used to 7.5 cm seams. A lockstitch machinist will usually learn other lockstitch operations faster than someone who has previously worked with an overlocker. It pays to identify the key difference. In the case of longer seams it is the fact that the left hand must keep moving, as the material advances, walking the fingers. For very short seams this is not necessary.

Points to watch

Habits
Good habits, once learned, are usually retained and so are bad habits! Trainees should learn the correct method in the beginning even if, as so often happens, it is a more difficult one to learn.

Targets
The clearer that we can see a target and the nearer that we are to attaining it, the harder we work. The final target is full competence but it is possible to set intermediate targets which can be reached in a few days. These can be an intermediate performance for the whole job, top performance for one part or a combination of the two.

Quality
Correct methods produce good quality; wrong methods may do so only at the expense of speed.

Punishment and rewards
Most readers will be familiar with the idea that training is improved if good work is praised, but it may also be helpful to admonish those few who are slack. However, harsh words and sarcasm can merely cause trainees to ignore the trainer. They may shut out the unpleasant sensation by not listening and in doing so set up a barrier to further learning.

Psychology of learning

The ideas set out above make good commonsense but they are also fully supported by the research of the psychologists. These have led to many detailed theories which are of great importance to training officers and others who must design and control training proprammes. Nevertheless, a supervisor who sticks to the simple principles, which have been listed, is unlikely to go far wrong.

Putting training to work

Management involvement in supervisor training

The best training in supervision is that from a very good boss. The subject has many subtle aspects, which are best taught in a practical context. Special courses are useful in order to introduce new ideas, provided that everybody attends and that they are fully backed by management. Sometimes a particular supervisor may have a special problem and a special course may help but only if the supervisor actively wants the course and gets 'on the job' coaching afterwards. For new supervisors a training course serves several purposes, only one of which is to provide a grounding in the basic theory.

The content of any course must accord with the principles on which the parent factory is run unless they are part of a wholesale change.

No training is any good unless managers understand what is to be taught, agree with it and actively support it. They must have a knowledge of the subject; sufficient for the selection of the trainees, the course content and (if possible) the trainers. The training of supervisors is only justified to the extent which it fits them to their present or future job in the industry. The rest is 'education' and another thing entirely.

The training of operatives

In the same way operatives should be trained to make them effective in the supervisor's section in order to increase its efficiency and so it is in their interest to help to ensure that it is done properly. Even when it is for a future post, as part of promotion, the good supervisor takes a pride in it going well.

When operatives are taken on with little skill, it would upset the balance of the lines and spoil quality if they were to be put straight into the sections. A special training centre overcomes this problem but close contact between supervisors, instructors and trainees is the only way to make sure that the training suits the practical needs of production.

There comes a stage in the training of all beginners when they are transferred to the section. Usually this is when their performance is between 75 and 100 BSI. If supervisors have got to know them whilst they were in the training centre they will be able to make them feel at home and to build on the training given there. In some factories there is an 'on the job' instructor who can help with this.

Style changes and so do machines. Most of the burden of the resultant retraining falls on the supervisor. Skill in this area can make a great deal of difference to balancing problems. Sometimes the supervisor may not have the sewing skills necessary to teach a particular skill and, if no specialist instructor is available, may have to work through an operative. Then training skills are even more necessary.

Preparation

Put the trainee at ease. State the job to be learned, check the trainee's existing knowledge and skills, in order to establish the starting point for instruction. Create interest in the job, to help to motivate the trainee to learn.

See that the work is ready and in the usual form. Make sure that the workplace and the machine are in good order. Adjust the seat etc. for the demonstration. If training aids or exercises are required, are they ready and is the instructor familiar with them? What are the quality standards?

Can the trainee(s) see and hear properly? If not, what can be done about it? If possible rehearse, especially if you are not used to instructing.

Presentation

Tell, show and illustrate as appropriate, so that use is made of as many of the trainee's senses as possible. *Teach one stage at a time.* This enables the trainee(s) to assimilate one bit of learning before going on to the next. They must always be given a chance to practise for some time at each stage in order for it to register permanently.

Instruct clearly, completely and patiently, demonstrating as required. Beware of jargon, which is not likely to be understood by a trainee. Avoid backtracking to put in forgotten items. Give only the essential information and at a suitable pace, with plenty of time for the trainee(s) to ask questions and to soak up the detail. The rate of instruction should suit the trainee's capacity to learn.

Trial run

Let the trainee(s) have a go as soon as possible. Use scrap material if necessary. It is a good way to retain interest and gives the instructor a chance to see how much more there is to be taught. Reassure and give praise whenever possible.

Demonstration

Show how it is done at speed but stop to cover key points. Demonstrate again, at speed, without stopping.

Practice and coaching

The trainee(s) can then tackle the job, doing one cycle, then several and after that for longer and longer periods. Encourage speed, since the method changes as pace slows. If you want to correct a point, stop the work. Once the method is roughly right, set speed targets. After the first attempts the trainees can practise alone or in pairs. Working in pairs has the advantage that one can relax between practice sessions and check on the other's performance, which in itself is a means of learning. For most sewing machinery it is wrong to teach more than two people at once.

Quality

It is best if the trainees' first efforts are made without reference to the quality standards achieved, since this would slow them down. At an early stage try for the correct quality on short runs. Never vary the acceptable quality level but avoid depressing trainees by harsh criticism. The use of scrap and the employment of other trainees in unpicking is recommended.

Follow up

When the trainees are becoming competent, look for minor points of skill. Make spot checks on quality. Take care that had habits do not slip in; the easiest way for a trainee is not necessarily the best one. Work towards the level of real skill, when they are looking forward towards the next element whilst finishing the one before.

Retraining

A working supervisor will be involved in extending and changing the skills of existing machinists rather than in training new staff, except in the final stages. This can best be done in short spells during the working day, often as part of balancing. Remember that experienced people may resent the lack of skill that makes retraining necessary. This applies particularly to people who have a poor record for quality or output.

Non-machinist training

For convenience, machinist training has been used as an example, but the same principles apply to all operatives and much of the training for other work. It requires little extension to apply to the training of supervisors in balancing and the like. Practical training by demonstration and coaching is rare, more because of a lack of confidence on the part of those responsible than because of any obvious disadvantage. Where, as is often the case, the instructor lacks the necessary practical skill, a mutual help exercise is recommended.

> Learning is the most exhausting of all jobs.

Leadership training

Everyone is different

Supervisor training in human relations has been plagued for years by oversimplifiers: people who draw up rules based partly on some experimental psychology and partly on their own limited experience. 'Just follow these rules and you will become the perfect supervisor.'

You cannot generalise in that way. Take ten workers and face each with the same situation and each will react differently. Take one worker and ten supervisors and each will take a different approach, suited to the individual personalities involved – that of the supervisor as well as that of the worker.

Training in people skills

If you cannot write down rules you can suggest guidelines, based on the reaction of the better supervisors to different situations. An attempt has been made earlier in this chapter. It is one thing to put such ideas on paper but it is another to persuade supervisors to use the suggested approaches.

We do not just *tell* machinists how to sew. We tell them, demonstrate, give them a chance to practise and coach them. There are difficulties in adopting this method with leadership training, not the least of which is that whilst instructors can easily demonstrate the superiority of their method of machining, it is less easy to do so for supervision. We can, however, give supervisors a chance to practise what we preach in the lecture room and then offer the criticism of their fellows.

Exercises

Set the group a practical task, preferably useful and related to their work. Appoint one as the supervisor. The 'supervisor' is then interviewed privately by an instructor, so that he or she can describe the 'people problems' encountered and how to overcome them. Meanwhile, the 'operatives' complete an anonymous analysis sheet. During the training session the instructor acts as a referee, in order that the 'operatives' do not behave too outrageously. If the atmosphere is right the 'supervisor's' confessional can be public. It is important not to allow this to develop into a slanging match. The spirit of friendly co-operation is vital to the success of the exercise. When every participant has had a turn, each is interviewed privately again, so that the feedback from the other trainees can be discussed. In a suitable climate the trainee's boss can be present on this occasion, in order that the feedback can be discussed in the light of the experiences of the factory.

An alternative approach, which is complementary, is to carry out the exercises with no formal leader.

Analysis forms

Leadership of such training sessions is not easy but some managers may wish to do the job themselves. In this case it is vital that the approach to the analysis forms is described carefully:

'These forms (Fig. 11.1) are designed so that you can note your assessment of the other members of your group easily and quickly. They are rather like the quizzes that you find in women's magazines, such as "Are you a good mother?" They should be completed carefully, since your colleagues will rely on them, in order to improve their skills. They will be doing the same for you.

'As a first exercise you should complete a form for what you regard as the perfect leader. You should put your name on this. At the end of the course we will ask you to give us a secret vote as to which of you did the best. We shall not tell you who that is but we will give you their average score. You can then compare it with the first form (Fig. 11.1).

'After the exercises please fill in a form for the person who was acting as 'supervisor'. You do not need to put your name on it and we shall not reveal what you personally have written. We shall merely produce an average score for each leader in turn.'

On some courses the 'supervisor' also completes a form for the 'operatives'.

> We learn from the advice of our friends, not our enemies.

No losers

Such training requires very skilled instructors, who are able to ensure that no one feels inadequate or is distressed by the experience. A vital part is the discussion of the 'leader/subordinate report' and its application to practical supervision. Half an hour is the bare minimum for this.

During the practical sessions the supervisors will exhibit modified behaviour as they seek to score well on the leader/subordinate marking. High scores will be equally well valued by those who seek most the approval of their peers and those who are more concerned with the boss.

> If leadership training is not enjoyable
> the instructor is a poor leader.

Leader/subordinate analysis

Quality	Explanation
Dominance	To what extent was the individual able to make themselves felt in the group? How successfully was prestige established and maintained and how? How much effort was put in?
Activity	To what extent did this person co-operate with the aims of the team?
Co-operation	With what conviction were the delegate's plans proposed and those of others criticised?
Self-confidence	Were the problems which were encountered confronted as if success was still assured?
Acceptablity	How well was the delegate accepted by the rest of the group?
Quality of thought	Regardless of whether the delegate's ideas were accepted, were they sensible?
Planning ability	To what extent was the delegate able to string ideas together into a proper plan?
Communication	How easily did the rest of the group understand the ideas put forward by the delegate?
Morale	What was the effect of the delegate on the morale of the group?
Objectivity	Were the ideas put forward based on the facts?

Leader/subordinate rating

Quality	Rating	Explanation
Dominance	5	All ideas accepted without discussion.
	4	Emerged as group leader.
	3	Respected.
	2	Often ignored.
	1	Disregarded.
Activity	5	Furiously busy.
	4	Works away at suitable tasks as they occur.
	3	Tackles some tasks and leaves some to others.
	2	Makes little contribution.
	1	Idle.
Co-operation	5	Total commitment
	1	Always went own way.
Self-confidence	5	'Bulldozer'.
	4	Statements made with authority.
	3	Statements made with diffidence.
	2	Easily discouraged.
	1	No personal ideas.
Acceptability	5	Greatly liked by all.
	1	Unpopular.
Quality of thought	5	Perfect ideas.
	1	Muddled thinker.
Planning ability	5	Foresees every difficulty.
	1	Takes everything as it comes.
Communication	5	Every idea expressed perfectly in the group's language.
	1	Incomprehensible.
Morale	5	Cheerful, smoothes out friction between others and gingers the group to high achievement.
	1	Pessimistic wet blanket, who delights in promoting strife.
Objectivity	5	Always seeks best method, regardless of personal popularity or loss of face.
	4	Speaks out for best method when it is important to do so.
	3	Usually sensible but inclined to favour the ideas of friends.
	2	Only certain types of ideas are acceptable. Only some members of the group able to influence.
	1	Bigoted.

N.B. Top marks are not necessarily the best.

NAMES	Dominance	Activity	Co-operation	Self confidence	Acceptability	Quality of thought	Planning ability	Communication	Morale	Objectivity

© Wrenbury Associates

* Delete as appropriate

Fig. 11.1 Leader/subordinate analysis: confidential score sheet.

The training plan for supervisors

Training needs analysis

It is useful for an outsider to monitor the performance of the individual supervisors at their work. Based on the supervisors' list of key problems, a schedule may be prepared of the skills which appear to be below the required level and priorities allocated. From this a course can be prepared which best meets the needs of the company.

Course content

Some of the supervisors' difficulties may be remedied by better management. Others may be reduced by training, provided that care is taken to avoid any implied criticism. A course which concentrates on problems which have been identified by the supervisors is likely to have their support.

Skills in dealing with people

Most of us learn by experience. That means that supervisors who have a similar background to their subordinates will have some advantages. However, some individuals will have learned wrong behaviour from their experience. A combination of simple theory and the help of their colleagues seems to be the most effective remedy.

Training check list

Training should be planned in advance. The nature of the plan will depend upon circumstances but a useful checklist is set out below.

• Who should be trained?	Skills inventory
• For what jobs?	" "
	New styles and machinery
	Poor quality
• Who will do the training?	Special skills
	Time available
	Shared responsibility
• Are there special exercises or aids?	
• Is a video camera available?	

12
Charting and Layouts

Introduction

Involving the supervisors

Conventionally the planning of factory layout is a task for senior management. However, if they consult with all the supervisors about the overall plan and actively involve every one of them in the detail of their section, not only will a better plan result but it will be more likely to be made to work by the supervisor. In fact it is always best to present a draft of the detailed section plan to the operatives concerned for much the same reasons.

Analysis by means of charts

A graphical display of a problem, where this is possible, eases the understanding of its nature. The strengths and weaknesses of a proposed solution are always more clearly exposed when it can be demonstrated graphically. This is particularly true where supervisors are concerned, for, whilst they may be as intelligent as management, they are less accustomed to using written words as a means of conveying information. Special symbols, the international ones of Work Study or those which are proposed for our industry, greatly simplify the presentation.

Charting individuals

Approaches such as the 'two-handed process chart' have a limited application but are included for the sake of completeness.

Charting factories

Here the chart comes into its own. The level of sophistication can stretch from an A4 print, with pencil lines substituting for string diagrams, to an 2.4 m × 1.2 m (8 ft by 4 ft) iron-faced panel with the symbols which represent operations or machinery mounted on magnets. Computers are less helpful for the purposes of presentation but can be utilised by the WSO at the planning stage.

Network analysis

This is a fairly sophisticated technique which is only likely to be employed successfully by those who possess some detailed technical training. It is particularly appropriate to complex layout planning and, for all but the simplest jobs, a suitable computer program is recommended.

Layout

The best layout for a given factory will depend upon a variety of factors:

- the minimum length of route for manual humping and expensive mechanical transportation;
- the machinery location, which may need to be near to services or where the floor is strong enough to bear its weight;
- the method of transportation, which may require straight lines, like a belt conveyor or to be graded downwards, like gravity-powered devices;
- the production system involved, especially in respect to the division between process and product layout;
- the type of garment being manufactured, which may or may not lend itself to parallel make or to detailed sectionalisation;
- the shape of the building and the number of its floors;
- safety requirements, such as that for the provision of adequate gangways.

Analysis by means of charts

The flow of work and the type of activity can be shown in a diagrammatic fashion by 'flow process charts'. These can be 'man type', 'material type' or 'equipment type'. They are often prepared by the WSO prior to layout planning and all members of management should familiarise themselves with the conventions, so that they can be used in discussions. Distance, quantity of movement and standard time for each operation may also be added.

Flow process charts

Numbers or letters may be placed within the symbols and symbols combined.

○	Operation, this is a main step in a process, method or procedure. It denotes change in the part, material or product.
▢	Inspection (Gilbreth for quantity only).
◇	Inspection for quality (Gilbreth only).
⇨	Transportation (except for Gilbreth who uses a small circle).
▽	Permanent storage.
▽ or D	Temporary storage or delay (ASME use D).
⊙	Combined activities, in this case operation and inspection.

Industry-related symbols

It is helpful to use special symbols to indicate different types of operation and those employed by the author are set out below. A flow chart with such symbols is particularly helpful for planning parallel make.

○	Hand operation.
	Flat bed sewing machine operation.
	Overlock sewing machine operation.
	Hand sewing operation.
⊙	Button sewing machine operation.
	Buttonholing machine operation.

☥   Power or hand pressing on bucks operation.

⊐   Hand iron as in underpressing operation.

S   Special machine operation.

F   Finishing operation.

Two-handed process charts

'This is a chart in which the activities of a worker's hands and/or limbs are recorded in their relationship to one another': *Introduction to Work Study*, International Labour Office.

The symbols are those described above for flow process charts. The chart is like the two-handed chart considered under 'Basic Work Study' but a central column is devoted to each form of activity. It is always best to divide the operation into elements and then to study one hand at a time for the whole of the element.

This technique is particularly useful to the engineer, since it helps to isolate those parts of the work cycle which can be performed automatically.
    An example of this type of chart is shown in Figure 12.1.

Outline process charts

These give an overall picture by recording only the main operations and inspections, each of which is numbered. The sequence is indicated by an arrow and a line which connects successive workstations, as shown in Fig. 12.2.

Network analysis

Its main application to layouts is in the reduction of throughput time. The basic principle is that if a job is split into parts it will take the least time if the longest part is started first. So, when we are cooking Sunday lunch, we prepare the joint and the potatoes for roasting first. Then we tackle the steamed pudding, after that the vegetables and finally the custard. If there is only one peeler we must prepare the carrots, parsnips and potatoes in sequence but someone else could be getting on with the pudding, the cabbage and the custard.

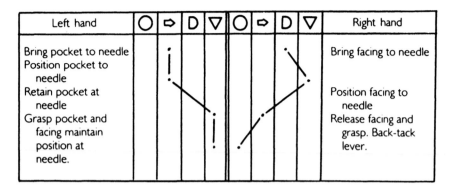

Left hand	○	⇨	D	▽	○	⇨	D	▽	Right hand

Bring pocket to needle
Position pocket to
  needle
Retain pocket at
  needle
Grasp pocket and
  facing maintain
  position at
  needle.
									Bring facing to needle
									
									Position facing to
									  needle
									Release facing and
									  grasp. Back-tack
									  lever.

Fig. 12.1 Example of a two-handed process chart.

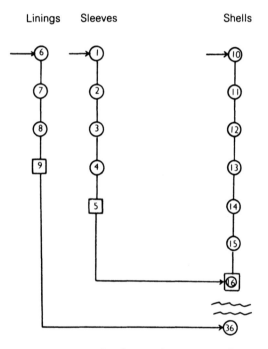

Fig. 12.2 Example of an outline process chart.

Layout

The Work Study function

The Work Study Officer will be expected to provide two sorts of assistance in the planning of factory layouts: the provision of suitable technical help, which assists management to make the correct decision, and the setting out of problems in a way that makes it easier for management to under-

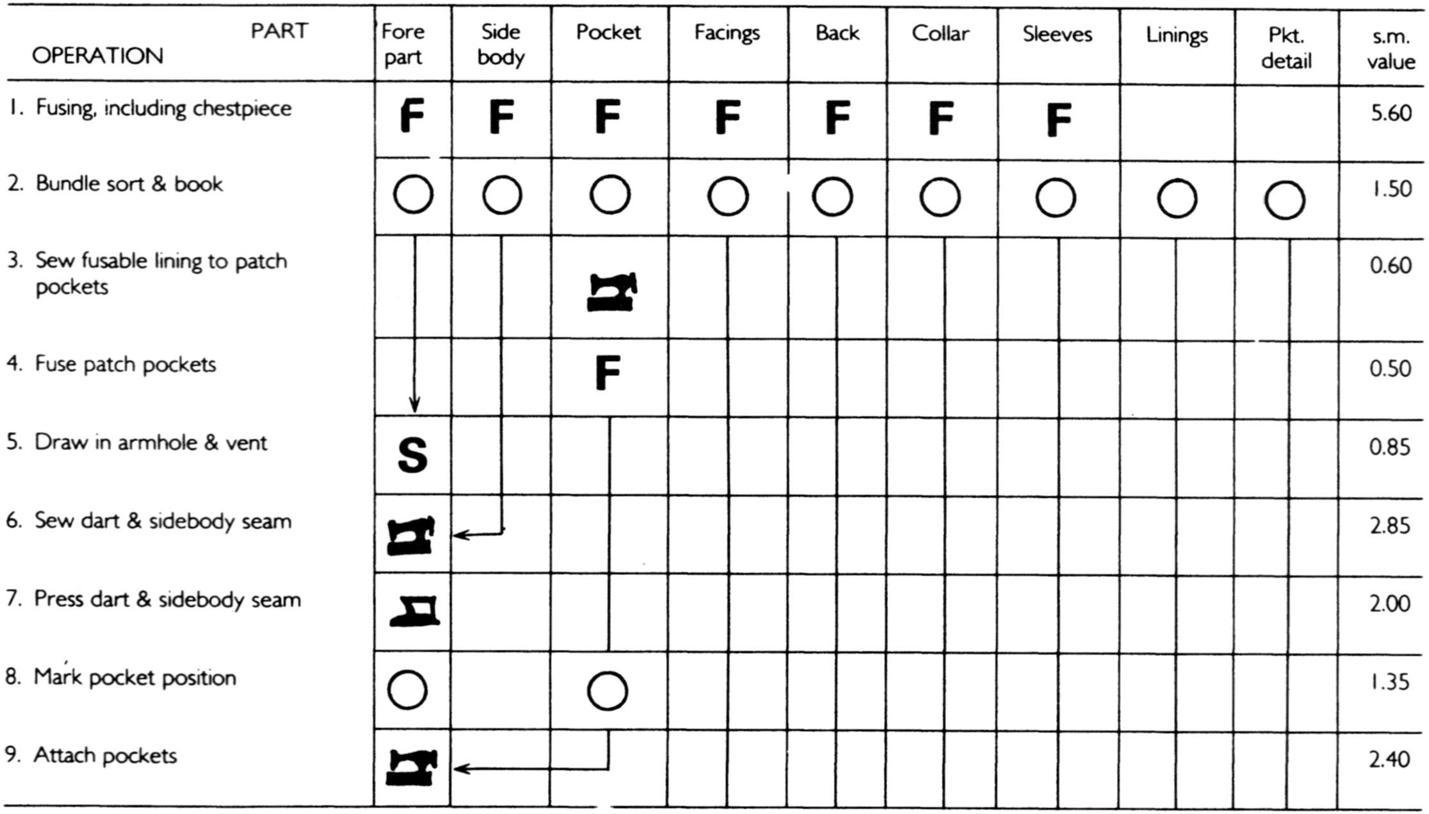

OPERATION / PART	Fore part	Side body	Pocket	Facings	Back	Collar	Sleeves	Linings	Pkt. detail	s.m. value
1. Fusing, including chestpiece	F	F	F	F	F	F	F			5.60
2. Bundle sort & book	O	O	O	O	O	O	O	O	O	1.50
3. Sew fusable lining to patch pockets			⛨							0.60
4. Fuse patch pockets			F							0.50
5. Draw in armhole & vent	S									0.85
6. Sew dart & sidebody seam	⛨									2.85
7. Press dart & sidebody seam	◁									2.00
8. Mark pocket position	O		O							1.35
9. Attach pockets	⛨									2.40

Fig. 12.3 The use of industry-related symbols in a flow chart.

stand them. The advantages of a graphical representation of a problem cannot be overemphasised. The more clearly that a problem is seen the better the solution is likely to be.

Management techniques

The use of the flow chart has already been described and an outline flow chart, such as that illustrated, is recommended in order to make a first decision about the order of make and if parallel manufacture is desirable. A 'string diagram', described below, is also useful after a tentative layout has been produced. Layouts should be of generous size, so that everyone can see what is proposed, and squared paper intended for a 'flip chart' (A2) is about right for most factories. Symbols, such as those on the flow chart, can be mounted on magnetic squares and the plan laid on a sheet of ferrous material. Then the 'machines' can be moved easily and are not likely to become dislodged. Suitable equipment is advertised in the Work Study magazines.

String diagrams

These can be used for a variety of purposes but in layout planning their most important use is in tracing the movement of a bundle. On a scale plan of the factory a thread follows its path.

The length of the thread used represents the scale distance travelled from the start to the finish of the production process or the part under consideration. In this way the distance which it has to travel for different layouts can be compared. For simple projects a pencil line, which traces the path, can do almost as well in indicating the gross errors of positioning. The thicker lines indicate multiple movement on one path as would several strands of string.

Specific locations for machinery

Some machinery can only be located in certain places:

Heavy machines
On the first and higher floors it may be necessary to use the corners or specially strengthened postions.

Services
Steam lines must be kept short, to avoid heat losses, but it may be economic for small volumes to use electric boilers.

High wattage electrical supply, vacuum and compressed air are similar.

Environment
Magnetic memory and computers should be kept away from stray electromagnetic fields, such as exist near high duty switches and transformers.

Fabrics will fade if exposed to strong sunlight and they must not be stored in a damp atmosphere. Fusing presses must be installed away from draughts.

Access
Some operations, like laying up, need to be accessible to forklift trucks, bringing up large bolts of cloth or other large and heavy items.

Transport

The means by which garments and parts are moved may affect the layout:

Belt conveyors
Straight lines are essential.

Manual humping
People power is expensive and its use must be restricted to small and light parts for short distances.

Gravity flow
If the roller conveyor, chute or rail is not in a straight line, then the gradient must be steeper.

Powered movement
If large quantities can be moved with little work by the operatives, then hauling over long distances may be acceptable.

Dynamic storage
Gravity or powered storage, usually on rails, is possible at a higher level than that normally used for work and so adds another dimentsion to layout.

Process versus product layout

Process layout
Similar operations and machines are grouped together (Fig. 12.4).

Product layout
Operations are grouped according to the type of garment manufactured, generally in order of make (Fig. 12.5).

Even where one type of garment is manufactured, processes of the same type can be grouped together with advantage. This approach is more flexible, since the absence of one operative or repairs for one operation will cause a smaller upset to balancing. Specialised sections, which feature one type of machine, become possible. The approach is becoming more attractive as high output automatics are introduced.

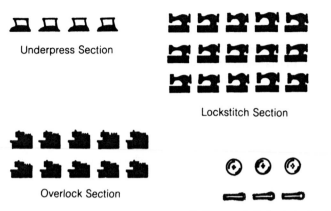

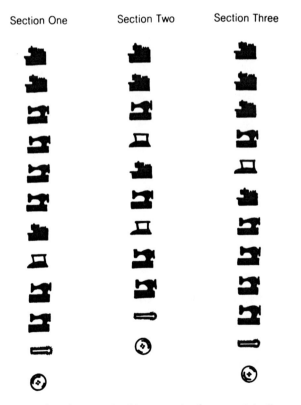

Fig. 12.4 Process layout.

Fig. 12.5 Product layout. (In this example, for a straight line system.)

Where a process layout is adopted, a low cost means of moving work between the groups of machines is essential, since work movement is inevitably increased. Greater supervisory skill is also essential. In consequence a product layout was more popular in the past. Where products were changed regularly the lines were rearranged to suit.

Production systems

The earlier production systems relied on 'manual humping' to move work or had simple aids such as conveyors. In consequence the physical position of workplaces was important. Now the introduction of automated mechanical handling has very much reduced the labour content of work movement and so the physical position of machinery is less important. Nevertheless, such a system is expensive and it is still vital to reduce the amount of track (and hence the distance travelled) to a minimum.

Style variation can affect the choice of production system in two ways. The sequence of operation will change and so will the work content from particular machines. The latter means that process layout may be better and all the orders will be processed by the factory as a whole. On the other hand the necessary flexibility may be achieved by using the automated mechanical handling systems or by ones where the lines may be rearranged quickly and cheaply, as with 'PBU baskets in racks'.

Parallel make

This is mentioned above but its applications are grouped here for convenience:
Fast throughput/sub-assemblies possible/small parts to large.

Exercise I

Required

Suggest an improved production system.
Redesign the factory layout and indicate a new flow of work.

Background

Product: Garments for infants and toddlers.
Fabric: Cotton and cotton synthetic mixtures, knitted on the premises and stored on rolls.
Cutting: Bandknife after sectioning with straight knife.
Motif: Fused to most garments.
'Splitting': Cut pieces are placed in box, each containing 36 garments.
Stitching sequence: Overlock edges, lockstitch, overlock as required.

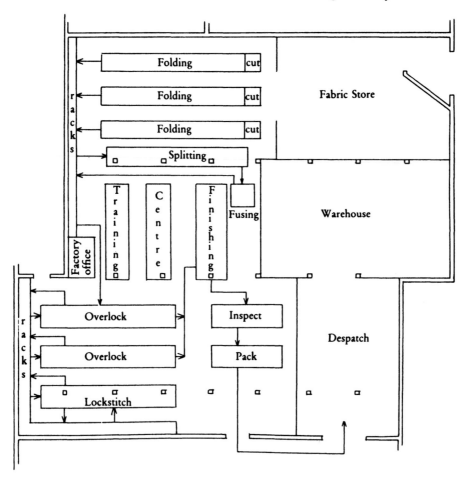

Fig. 12.6 Existing factory layout for Exercise 1.

Finishing: Press studs or button/buttonhole closure, examine, pack and then to store in warehouse.
Work movement: In boxes manually.

Figure 12.6 shows the existing factory layout. Figure 12.7 shows the proposed layout.

Answer to Exercise I

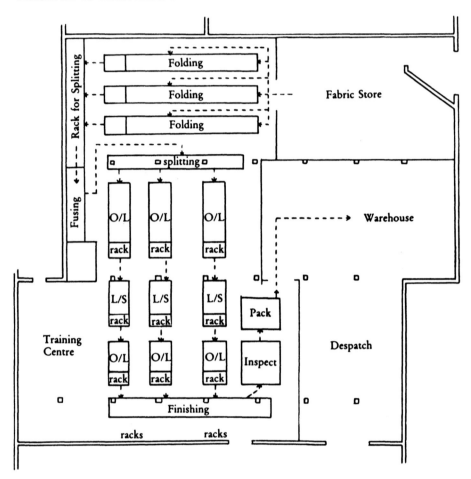

Fig. 12.7   Proposed factory layout for Exercise 1.

Exercise 2

Prepare a flow diagram for the present system.
Draw a 'string diagram' on the plan of the existing layout.
Prepare a new flow diagram and from this develop a new layout.
Figure 12.8 shows the existing factory layout and Fig. 12.9 shows the
current sewing room layout. Tables 12.1 and 12.2 provide the key to the
sewing room layout and the operation sequence for jackets respectively.
No answer is provided.

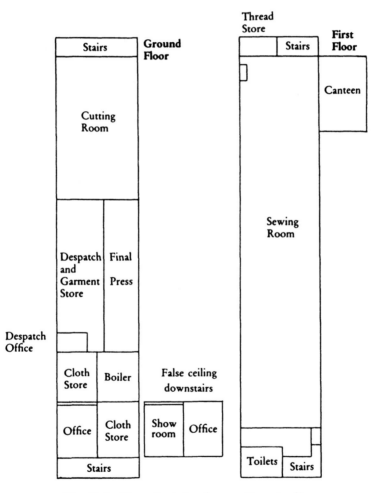

Fig. 12.8   Plan of existing factory (Exercise 2).

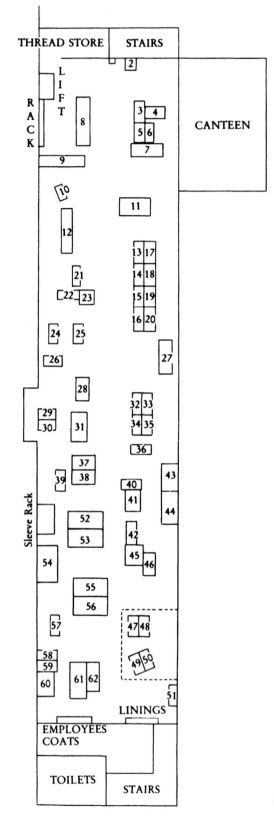

Fig. 12.9 Current sewing room layout.

Table 12.1   Key to current sewing room layout.

Workplace No.	Workplace	Operation* No.
1.	Lightning fasteners zip slider and stopper attachment	trs.
2.	Closing M/C for attaching trouser prongs and bars	trs.
3.	Pfaff Lockstitch	trs.
4.	Singler button M/C	trs.
5.	Leo Bremman Blind Stitch	trs.
6.	Wilcox and Gibbs Overlocker	trs.
7.	Trouser table	trs.
8.	Table	1
9.	Table	45
10.	Sussman small parts press new not yet connected	–
11.	Table	trs.
12.	Finishing Table	42 & 43
13.	Pfaff Lockstitcher	trs.
14.	Pfaff Lockstitcher	trs.
15.	Pfaff Lockstitcher	trs.
16.	Pfaff Lockstitcher	trs.
17.	Pfaff Lockstitcher	trs.
18.	Pfaff Lockstitcher	trs.
19.	Jones Lockstitcher Not in use	–
20.	Pfaff Lockstitcher	trs.
21.	Bellow chain baste rarely used	–
22.	Pfaff bar tack	trs.
23.	Reece Button Hole Machine	44
24.	Pfaff Lockstitcher pad insert	41
25.	Pfaff Lockstitcher differential feed	38
26.	Pfaff Lockstitcher cylinder machine bed	38
27.	Vacuum pressing table with Ibis steam iron and sleeve board	6
28.	Booth pressing unit, with shoulder bucks and steam iron	13, 29 & 39
29.	Pfaff lockstitcher	Vests
30.	Pfaff Lockstitcher	30
31.	Bellows 'Hoffman type' press	21, 26 & 31
32.	Pfaff Lockstitcher	8
33.	Pfaff Lockstitcher	5
34.	Pfaff Lockstitch Zig–Zag machine	7
35.	Pfaff Lockstitcher	20
36.	Pfaff Lockstitch Zig–Zag machine with a split foot	16
37.	Table	22
38.	Table	22
39.	Pfaff Lockstitcher	35
40.	Bellows Blindstitcher	15 & 25
41.	Pfaff Plonker Baster	14 & 24
42.	Pfaff Chainstitcher	23
43.	Aspiromat vacuum pressing table with Ibis steam iron	9
44.	Aspiromat vacuum pressing table with Sussman steam iron	4

Table 12.1 *Continued*

Workplace No.	Workplace	Operation* No.
45.	Reece pocket jetting machine	2 & 10
46.	Bundle table for Reece M/C	2 & 10
47.	Pfaff Lockstitcher	3
48.	Pfaff Lockstitcher	11
49.	Bellow Blindstitcher rarely used	–
50.	Pfaff Lockstitcher	3
51.	Singer L/S not in use	–
52.	Table	34, 36 & 40
53.	Table	37 & 32
54.	Table	33
55.	Table	19
56.	Table	27
57.	Pfaff Lockstitcher	12 & 28
58.	Bellow Ch/St not in use	–
59.	Pfaff M/C table, not in use	–
60.	Booth trouser pressing bucks, not in use	–
61.	Table	18
62.	Table	18

* Cross reference to 'Operation sequence for jackets' (Table 12.2).

Table 12.2 Operation sequence for jackets.

Operation No.	Operation	Workplace* No.
1.	Bundles sorted and booked	8
2.	Lining in breast pockets jetted	45
3.	Make lining including inside pockets	47 & 50
4.	Lining press	44
5.	Make sleeves	33
6.	Press sleeves	27
7.	Attach melton to conventional collars	34
8.	1st sew, sew darts, centre back seam, make flaps	32
9.	Press	43
10.	Pockets jetted	45
11.	2nd sew, make outside pockets	48
12.	Close side seams	57
13.	Press	28
14.	Insert canvas	41
15.	Lash bridle	40
16.	Machine down corners of front breast welt pocket, using monofilament translucent thread	36
17.	Downstairs to press on 'hoffman type' shaped body press	–

Table 12.2 *Continued*

Operation No.	Operation	Workplace* No.
18.	Match in lining	61 & 62
19.	Baste facings, mark lapels shape and trim hem	55
20.	Sew round front edge attach linings to shell and tape	35
21.	Press edges	31
22.	Trim turnout front edge and baste lapel corners	37 & 38
23.	Edge baste fronts, collar and hem	42
24.	Plonker baste facing	41
25.	Blind stitch the facing and hem	40
26.	Press edges	31
27.	Trim armholes, lining, collar and mark collar points	56
28.	Close shoulders	57
29.	Press shoulders	28
30.	Attach collar and make all non-standard collars	30
31.	Press collar	31
32.	Baste under collar for felling	53
33.	Fell back collar corners and catch down collar on inside	54
34.	Trim vents	52
35.	Machine vents	39
36.	Baste top of vents for felling	52
37.	Match in sleeves	53
38.	Insert sleeves, sleeves are basted if necessary to relieve bottleneck	52 25 & 26
39.	Press sleeve head	28
40.	Baste round armhole	52
41.	Insert pad and wadding	24
42.	Felling sleeve head lining, vents and under collar	12
43.	Baste palling	12
44.	Button holes	23
45.	Brushing off trim thread ends	9
46.	Downstairs for pressing off and button sewing	

* Cross reference to 'Current sewing room layout' (Fig. 12.9).
Workplaces 1–7, 11 and 13–22 are trouser section workplaces only.
Workplace 29 is used for make-through vests.

Reading List

General

Carr, H. and Latham, B. (1994) *The Technology of Clothing Manufacture*. Oxford, Blackwell Science.
Cooklin, G. (1991) *Introduction to Clothing Manufacture*. Oxford, Blackwell Science.

Work study

ILO (1992) *Introduction to Work Study*. International Labour Office.

Production Systems Planning and Control

Taylor, P. (1990) *Computers in the Fashion Industry*. Heinemann Professional Publishing.
Tyler, D. (1991) Materials Management in Clothing Production. Oxford, Blackwell Science.

Total Quality Control

Price, F. (1989) *Right First Time*. Aldershot, Gower Publishing Company.
Crosby, P.H. (1983) *Quality is Free*. Mentor Publishing.

Charting and Layouts

Lockyer, K.G. (1991) in *Critical path analysis and other project techniques*, edited by J. Gordan. London, Pitman.

Index

Activity, 104
Allowances, 49 *et seq.*
Analysis by means of charts, 167 *et seq.*
ASME (American Society of Mechanical
    Engineers), 169

Bags, 95
Balance control, 66
Balancing, 55 *et seq.*
Balancing (category of off standard time),
    20
Band knives, 132
Basic time, 51, 52
Baskets, 96
Belt conveyors, 100, 174
Bottleneck operations, 70
Boxes, 96
Breakpoints, 31, 42
Bundle trucks, 97

Clamps
    on cords, 96
    on rails, 96
Capacity
    calculations, 106
    inventory, 107
Central storage, 98, 99, 100
Chutes, 97
Cloth inspection, 124
Communication, 2, 148, 149
Computerisation, 101, 108
Contingency allowance, 50
Courtesy, 44

Critical path, 106
Customer returns (RTM's), 139
Cutting, 128 *et seq.*

Decimal stopwatches, 41
Direct costs, 13, 15
Discipline, 7, 144, 150
Drills, 131

EAD, 27
Effect of changeover, 106
Efficiency, 14, 17
Electronic boards, 41, 42
Elements, 43, 59
Event, 104
Excess work content, 14

Factory
    quality specifications, 118
    routine, 8
Fatigue allowance, 50
Fitness for purpose, 113
Flexible Intermediate Examination, 102
Floater, 56, 62, 64, 66, 69
Flyback
    timing, 44
    watches, 40
Form presses, 137
Fusibles, 127
Fusing presses, 127

Garment
    engineering, 17
    synthetics, 37

Garment Sewing Data (GSD), 53
Gilbreth (F.B. Gilbreth) symbols, 169
Grading, 47
Groups, 145 *et seq.*

Heads and bucks, 137
HOIL (How output is lost), 13 *et seq.*

Induction, 6
Ineffective time, 44
Initial
  balance, 62, 78, 93
  manning, 64
Interflow, 99, 100, 101
Inspection methods (cloth and
    trimmings), 126
Intermediate examination, 134
Intrinsic work content, 15

Job knowledge, 156
Just In Times (JIT), 110

Key quality features, 124
Key Result Areas, 10
Kinaesthesia, 155

Laying up, 129
Leadership, 145
  training, 155, 169 *et seq.*
Learning, 155
Live storage, 100

Machine delay
  allowance, 50
  (category of 'off standard time'), 19
Materials Requirements Planning (MRP),
  109
Manufacturing Resource Planning (MRP
  II), 110
Management information, 9
Managerial excess, 16
Manual dexterity, 156
Marking in, 129
Method study, 7, 23
Minimum order size, 106
MISSCHURN, 29
Money
  costs, 8
  wages, 8
Moulding, 137

NACERAP (FACERAP), 118
Network analysis, 168
Normalised time, 170

Observed rating (observed rate), 47, 48,
  51
Off standard work (off standard), 13, 17,
  19
On standard work (on standard), 13
Operation breakdown, 59, 60, 74
Operative
  efficiency, 17, 18
  performance, 17, 19, 39
Operator training (operative training),
  156 *et seq.*
Outline process charts, 170
Overheads, 13
Overhead rails, 100, 101

Patrol examination, 135
Pattern engineering, 124
Performance (operative), 17, 19, 39
Personal allowance, 50
Planning, 105
Plant
  quality level, 116
  throughput time, 107
Pocketed bags, 96
Policy excess (work content), 14
Potential production, 15
Powered tools (for cutting), 130
Predetermined Motion Time Systems
  (PMTS), 53 *et seq.*
Predicted
  attendance, 59
  performance, 59
  utilisation, 59
Pressing, 137
Principles of motion economy, 29
Process controlled work content, 14
Process versus product layout, 178
Production
  capacity, 107
  checks, 68
  planning and control, 102 *et seq.*
  planning, scheduling and control, 105
    et seq.
  systems, 94 *et seq.*, 174, 176
Progressive line or synchroflow, 73, 98
Psychology of learning, 157
Purchasing (cloth and trimmings), 125

Quality, 4, 5, 6, 39, 111 *et seq.*
  audit, 138
  characteristics, 123
  checks, 11
  control department, 113
  cycle, 143
  specifications, 104

Rail, 98
Rating, 39, 47 *et seq.*
Rejects (category of 'off standard time'),
  20
Repairs (category of 'off standard time'),
  20
'Right First Time', 114, 122
Roller conveyor, 96
Round knives, 130

Safety, 87
SATRA conveyor (central storage), 99
Samples (category of 'off standard time'),
  20
Sampling, 111, 114, 135
Scheduling, 58
Sealed samples, 141
Seam pucker, causes of, 136
Section efficiency, 17
Sectionalisation, 56, 94
Selector type flow system, 99
Senses, 155
Skills (skill)
  centre, 107
  inventory, 56, 62, 63, 67, 76, 107
  rating, 49
  transfer, 157
Split hand (split action) watch, 40
Standard
  minutes (sm), 14, 15, 39, 49, 52
  performance, 39
  time, 51, 52
  work content, 14, 15
Statistical quality control, 114
Steam tunnels, 137
Storage (cloth and trimmings), 126
Straight knives, 131
Straight line or conveyor production flow,
  98

String diagrams, 173
Style allowance, 50
Supervisory duties, 1, 2, 6
Supervisor training needs, 10 *et seq.*
Supervisors' check list, 2
Synchroflow or progressive line, 98

Testing (cloth and trimmings), 125
Theoretical operation balance (theoretical
  balance), 56, 59, 61, 78, 79
Thread change allowance, 50
Time study, 38 *et seq.*
  sequence, 37
Timing, 44 *et seq.*
Tolerances, 117, 118
Training, 154, *et seq.*
  (category of 'off standard time'), 20
Transporter, 58
Treatment (cloth and trimmings), 126
Types of element, 43

Underpressing, 137
Unmeasured work (category of 'off
  standard time'), 20
Utilisation, 7, 17, 64, 72 *et seq.*

Value analysis, 123

Waiting time (category of 'off standard
  time'), 20
Waste percentage, 106
Watch rating, 48
Watches, 40 *et seq.*
Work
  aids, 136
  content, 15
  in process (work in progress) (WIP), 57,
    66, 70, 95, 103, 105
  measurement, 37
  Study, 19, 23 *et seq.*
    (category of 'off standard time'), 20
    function (charting and layouts), 171

'Zero defect', 114

Also available from Blackwell Publishing

Metric Pattern Cutting
Third Edition
Winifred Aldrich
The number one, best-belling book on pattern
cutting for women's wear, including a new
section on computerised pattern cutting and
numerous blocks.
ISBN 0 632 03612 5

Metric Pattern Cutting for Menswear
Including Computer Aided Design
Third Edition
Winifred Aldrich
In the third edition of this standard work on the
subject, sizing charts have been updated and the
chapter devoted to computer-aided design has
been updated and extended. An extra section on
workwear has been added.
ISBN 0 632 04113 7

**Metric Pattern Cutting for Children's
Wear and Babywear**
Third Edition
Winifred Aldrich
Another bestseller by Winifred Aldrich,
providing a simple but comprehensive system of
pattern cutting for children's wear and
babywear. Highly illustrated with hundreds of
stylish diagrams and clear, concise instructions.
ISBN 0 632 05265 1

**Pattern Cutting for Lingerie, Beachwear
and Leisurewear**
Ann Haggar
Describes the whole process from planning to
finished pattern pieces. Includes examples,
working diagrams and drawings and patterns
for stretch fabrics.
ISBN 0 632 02033 4

Dress Pattern Designing
The Basic Principles of Cut and Fit
Fifth Edition
Natalie Bray
With Fashion Supplement by Ann Haggar
This classic book contains over 100 basic
diagrams and 40 plates, combined with clear,
detailed instructions.
ISBN 0 632 01881 X

More Dress Pattern Designing
Fourth Edition
Natalie Bray
With Fashion Supplement by Ann Haggar
Expands the basic course, applying the
principles and methods to more advanced styles
and specialist cutting techniques. Includes
lingerie, tailoring and children's patterns.
ISBN 0 632 01883 6

Pattern Cutting for Women's Outerwear
Gerry Cooklin
An innovative book on pattern cutting
emphasising the technological aspects of pattern
development for women's mass-produced
clothing. An integrative method of drafting
block patterns is demonstrated, followed by a
wide-ranging tool-box of professional pattern
cutting techniques with many examples of their
applications.
ISBN 0 632 03797 0

Pattern Grading for Women's Clothes
The Technology of Sizing
Gerry Cooklin
Provides over 50 demonstrations of master and
basic garment grades, simple, clear instructions,
200 illustrations and 30 detailed charts of
international sizing systems.
ISBN 0 632 02295 7

Pattern Grading for Children's Clothes
The Technology of Sizing
Gerry Cooklin
Includes demonstration grades broken down
into illustrated stages with simple, clear
instructions, and children's size charts from
Europe and the USA.
ISBN 0 632 02612 X

Pattern Grading for Men's Clothes
Gerry Cooklin
A comprehensive manual of the practical
principles and applications of pattern grading
for the whole range of men's clothing, including
computerised grading, latest developments in
fully automatic grading and grades for linings,
fusibles and pockets.
ISBN 0 632 03305 3

**Introduction to Clothing Production
Management**
Second Edition
A J Chuter
Details fundamentals of quality control, fault
prevention, work study, effective supervision,
training, balancing, layouts and other
information essential for profitable operation.
ISBN 0 632 03939 6

The Technology of Clothing Manufacture
Second Edition
Harold Carr & Barbara Latham
Includes cutting, sewing, alternative methods of
joining materials and pressing; manual,
mechanical and computer-controlled methods
of production; current applications of
computerised techniques and robotics.
ISBN 0 632 03748 2

Materials Management in Clothing Production
D J Tyler
Discusses efficient control of materials emphasising key areas for production control principles for purchasing fabrics; material requirements planning; information technology for communications between suppliers and customers.
ISBN 0 632 02896 3

Fashion Design and Product Development
Harold Carr & John Pomeroy
Sets out the modern, commercial approach and discusses practical factors including materials, manufacture, costs, quality and organisation of the process.
ISBN 0 632 02893 9

Introduction to Clothing Manufacture
Gerry Cooklin
This introductory textbook explains practical aspects of manufacture, from original design to deliveries to retailers; basic planning and manufacturing technologies; and contains realistic examples of the daily operations of a clothing factory.
ISBN 0 632 02661 8

Knitted Clothing Technology
Terry Brackenbury
Covers specific techniques used to convert weft knitted fabric into garments, techniques for shaping and construction, specialist assembly machinery, and future trends.
ISBN 0 632 02807 6

Fashion Source Book
Kathryn McKelvey
This comprehensive source book offers fashion students a wealth of visual information to assist them in creating and presenting their design ideas. Over 1600 illustrations provide working drawings of garments, accessories and their details which can be used for reference whilst designing.
ISBN 0 632 03993 0

Fabric, Form, and Flat Pattern Cutting
Winifred Aldrich
The relationship between garment cut and fabric potential is probably the most important feature of present design skill. This book is based on an appraisal of the fabric and the body form to help students develop an intuitive and practical approach.
ISBN 0 632 03917 5

Dress Fitting
Second Edition
Natalie Bray
Discusses fitting problems including techniques for better fit; problems of figure, pastures and pattern adjustment; identifying and dealing with a defect.
ISBN 0 632 01879 8

Fashion Marketing
Second edition
Edited by Mike Easey
Marketing has been recognised only in the last decade as an indispensible component of fashion and clothing courses. The first edition (published in 1995) was written to satisfy student's requirements and has been revised to reflect changes in the fashion industry and in the development of fashion marketing practice.
ISBN 0 632 05199 X

Master Patterns and Grading for Women's Outsizes
Gerry Cooklin
The outsize market today consists of younger and more fashion-conscious women and there is a growing demand for well-designed clothes. This unique textbook provides up-to-date, practical information.
ISBN 0 632 03915 9

Illustrating Fashion
Kathryn McKelvey and Janine Munslow
The most important skill that fashion students need to communicate their ideas is the ability to create their own fashion illustrations. This contemporary and highly effective textbook sets out everything needed to master essential techniques.
ISBN 0 632 04024 6

Garment Technology for Fashion Designers
Gerry Cooklin
This handbook is designed to provide students and professionals with the fundamental principles of clothing technology in relation to their own work of design, pattern cutting and supervision of a sample making section.
ISBN 0 632 04775 5

Blackwell Publishing

A detailed catalogue with order form is available, on request, from:
Blackwell Publishing, 9600 Garsington Road, Oxford OX4 2DQ, UK
Telephone: 01865 776868 Fax 01865 714591

Lightning Source UK Ltd.
Milton Keynes UK
UKOW042134190911

178917UK00002B/3/P